SAGE was founded in 1965 by Sara Miller McCune to support the dissemination of usable knowledge by publishing innovative and high-quality research and teaching content. Today, we publish over 900 journals, including those of more than 400 learned societies, more than 800 new books per year, and a growing range of library products including archives, data, case studies, reports, and video. SAGE remains majority-owned by our founder, and after Sara's lifetime will become owned by a charitable trust that secures our continued independence.

Los Angeles | London | New Delhi | Singapore | Washington DC | Melbourne

Advance Praise

We often treat critical thinking and creativity as two separate disciplines. The research behind Creative Aerobics shows they are two sides of the same coin.

Eric J. Barron
President, The Pennsylvania State University

Whole-brained thinking is the need of the hour. Being slotted into either a 'Right Brain' or a 'Left Brain' individual is pretty much a limitation today. Creative Aerobics is a simple methodology to help you progress on the path to becoming a 'Whole-Brained' individual. A way to awaken the creative gene that manifests itself in every one of us. Creative Aerobics is one of the key self-development and progress mantras.

Madhukar Kamath
Group CEO and MD, DDB Mudra Group, India

Today's society wants to put up a barrier between art and science—which is very limiting to both—while also putting an emphasis on only developing STEM topics. This is exactly the opposite of what we need to be doing; curiosity in science is rooted in creativity—and art is enhanced by skills. Harnessing this combination of science and art is extremely powerful, and it can be further developed through creative aerobic exercises.

Matt MacBeth
CEO and Co-founder, Pi Lab; Creator of Edwin the Duck

Creativity in its own uncanny way makes humans put all of their brainpower to solve most complex problems. Often the ideas are unbiased, visionary, and create a path for achieving the impossible. If we wait for extraordinary circumstances to drive us to be creative, we would not innovate at the pace of human needs. What if we infuse a habit-forming way of thinking like creative aerobics—the potential could be endless, to unleash the creative power of many, sustainably, to build the muscle of creative thinking.

Malavika Melkote
Director, Information Technology, Fortune 500 Company

Creative Aerobics seems like 'magic', but it's real. Even those of my students who say they just are not creative get excited about producing clever and effective slogans and jingles with ease. They're able to do that after they learn to connect the analytical and creative sides of their brains through Creative Aerobics. It's easy, anybody can do it, and it's just the 'trick' for effective promotions.

Dr Susan Gonders
Professor, Southeast Missouri State University

Launch a satellite into outer space.
Pose a question to the mind.
Is there a difference?

As Linda and Arpan take us aboard on a remarkable journey of self-discovery, get ready to unravel creativity from within the deepest crevices of your mind, harness its power, and see magic unfold.

Monica Datta
A tiny speck in this vast, wonderful universe

CREATIVE AEROBICS

CREATIVE AEROBICS

Fueling Imagination in the 21st Century

Linda Conway Correll George

Arpan Yagnik

Los Angeles | London | New Delhi
Singapore | Washington DC | Melbourne

Copyright © Linda Conway Correll George and Arpan Yagnik, 2017

All rights reserved. No part of this book may be reproduced or utilized in any form or by any means, electronic or mechanical, including photocopying, recording, or by any information storage or retrieval system, without permission in writing from the publisher.

First published in 2017 by

SAGE Publications India Pvt Ltd
B1/I-1 Mohan Cooperative Industrial Area
Mathura Road, New Delhi 110 044, India
www.sagepub.in

SAGE Publications Inc
2455 Teller Road
Thousand Oaks, California 91320, USA

SAGE Publications Ltd
1 Oliver's Yard, 55 City Road
London EC1Y 1SP, United Kingdom

SAGE Publications Asia-Pacific Pte Ltd
3 Church Street
#10-04 Samsung Hub
Singapore 049483

Published by Vivek Mehra for SAGE Publications India Pvt Ltd, typeset in 11/14 pt Adobe Caslon Pro by Diligent Typesetter India Pvt Ltd, Delhi, and printed at Saurabh Printers Pvt Ltd, Greater Noida.

Library of Congress Cataloging-in-Publication Data

Names: George, Linda Conway Correll, author. | Yagnik, Arpan, author.
Title: Creative aerobics : fueling imagination in the 21st century / Linda Conway Correll George, Arpan Yagnik.
Description: Thousand Oaks, California : SAGE, 2017. | Includes bibliographical references and index.
Identifiers: LCCN 2017021829 (print) | LCCN 2017032591 (ebook) | ISBN 9789386446848 (E-Book) | ISBN 9789386446909 (E pub 2.0) | ISBN 9789386446824 (pbk : alk. paper)
Subjects: LCSH: Creative ability in business. | Creative ability. | Creative thinking.
Classification: LCC HD53 (ebook) | LCC HD53 .G465 2017 (print) | DDC 658.4/094—dc23
LC record available at https://lccn.loc.gov/2017021829

ISBN: 978-93-864-4682-4 (PB)

SAGE Team: Manisha Mathews, Tapajyoti Chaudhuri, Madhurima Thapa and Rajinder Kaur

Dedications

This book is dedicated to my mentor Tony Isidore, Copywriter/Copy Supervisor/Copy Chief at Young & Rubicam Advertising (Y&R) in New York City when I was a Time Records Clerk there. Tony gave me two advertising assignments: a Goodyear Tires print ad and a jingle to introduce Beech-Nut Fruit Stripe Gum. With his help, I was promoted to Copywriter in less than a year.

Tony's work is widely known in the United States. He wrote the 'Give a Damn' political campaign for the New York Urban Coalition that put John Lindsay in City Hall. In 1971, he left Y&R to form his own agency, Isidore Lefkowitz Elgort. Isidore & Paulson, The Larosa Isidore Group, and the Isidore Group followed. Tony is retired, but I'm sure he is still mentoring.

Linda Conway Correll George

My work in this book is dedicated to *Better Questions*!

Dr Arpan Yagnik

Thank you for choosing a SAGE product!
If you have any comment, observation or feedback,
I would like to personally hear from you.
Please write to me at **contactceo@sagepub.in**

Vivek Mehra, Managing Director and CEO, SAGE India.

Bulk Sales

SAGE India offers special discounts
for purchase of books in bulk.
We also make available special imprints
and excerpts from our books on demand.

For orders and enquiries, write to us at

Marketing Department
SAGE Publications India Pvt Ltd
B1/I-1, Mohan Cooperative Industrial Area
Mathura Road, Post Bag 7
New Delhi 110044, India

E-mail us at **marketing@sagepub.in**

Get to know more about SAGE

Be invited to SAGE events, get on our mailing list.
Write today to **marketing@sagepub.in**

This book is also available as an e-book.

Contents

Preface		ix
Acknowledgments		xv
Chapter 1:	Taking the Wraps/Raps off Creative Aerobics	1
Chapter 2:	In the Beginning ...	7
Chapter 3:	David versus Goliath, AKA Small versus The Big Idea	13
Chapter 4:	Defining the Creative Process Today	24
Chapter 5:	Developing Your Creative Magnifying Glass	31
Chapter 6:	Training for Your Creativity Marathon	39
Chapter 7:	Creative Aerobic 1 (CA1)—The Facts. Just the Facts	42
Chapter 8:	Creative Aerobic 2 (CA2)—New Nomenclature—It Is What It Isn't	51
Chapter 9:	Creative Aerobic 3 (CA3)—It's the Same. Only Different	59
Chapter 10:	Creative Aerobic 4 (CA4)—Refining Defining	65
Chapter 11:	Verbal Four-/For-/Foreplay	74
Chapter 12:	Body English (It's Not Just About Golf)	81
Chapter 13:	How the Student Award Winners Do It	96
Chapter 14:	How the Professionals Do It	109
Chapter 15:	Every Body (Copy) Needs a Slogan, Sometime	119
Chapter 16:	Mass Media Medley	128
Chapter 17:	.Com Creativity	140
Chapter 18:	Practical Reflections on the Profession	145
Index		156

Preface

The summer after my first year of teaching in the Advertising Department of the University of Florida, I had the opportunity to return to my first love, chronologically—the creative department of a multinational advertising agency located in Houston, Texas.

My time there was both an eye-opener and a mind-bender!

When I started in advertising in New York City years ago, television commercial ideas were hand-drawn by a bullpen of artists who did nothing but sketch storyboards—a series of illustrations that indicated the sequential action of the idea being presented, with the advertised product being introduced where appropriate. This could take a couple of days, or up to a week, depending on how busy the bullpen was. And it was always a rough approximation of what the commercial would actually look like.

Now, 21st-century television commercial concepts were being constructed, often the same day, for internal presentation, from existing footage found on the Internet, in news clips, on YouTube, and/or from films. And they looked like finished commercials!

Print ads were also the provenance of the art director now, not the bullpen, who, using digital programs like Illustrator and Photoshop, could create a ready-for-presentation ad in the matter of an hour or two.

Obviously, advertising's timetable had sped up considerably. It was on the express track, not the local. And it made me feel all the more certain that there is an increasing need today for a creative process that can keep pace. I think it's Creative Aerobics (CA), an ideation process I developed for my university students to make coming up with ideas faster, less stressful, and more fun.

Maybe you're ready to make a leap of faith and adopt the four exercises of CA that this book will teach you as your new ideation mantra. Or maybe you need to learn more about the process before you decide.

I've been presenting CA internationally, since 2003. Let me tell you how college academics and business professionals worldwide have responded to it. CA has been accepted for presentation on four continents, in juried international conferences at Monash University, Prato, Italy; Cambridge University, Cambridge, England, the United Kingdom; Carthage University, Tunis, Tunisia; American University, Paris, France; the First AIMS International Conference, Bangalore, India; the Fourth International Conference on Interdisciplinary Social Sciences, Athens, Greece; and the Eighth Annual Hawaii International Conference on Social Sciences, Honolulu. Also, it has been taught at universities and practiced internationally in India (Mumbai, Kolkata, Ahmedabad, New Delhi, Pune, etc.), Singapore, and the Emirates (Dubai).

Are you wondering what 'juried' means? To gain acceptance at conferences, the author and/or presenter has to write a short synopsis of the topic to be presented—CA, in this case. The synopsis, called an abstract, is submitted to scholarly organizations within a specific field—advertising, sociology, the humanities, for instance—that hold annual meetings where new ideas are introduced and shared with colleagues. If the evaluators of the abstracts deem the topics innovative and relevant, they are accepted. My CA abstracts have been accepted for presentation each time they've been submitted.

Often, after my presentations, invitations from international institutes of learning have followed: I presented CA at a lecture in the Distinguished Lecturer on Creativity Series at the National Institute of Design, Ahmedabad, India, the country's leading design institute. I made invited presentations at ICFAI Business School, Ahmedabad, India; at Osmania University, Hyderabad, India; Nirma University, Ahmedabad, India; Gujarat University, Ahmedabad, India; and Mumbai Educational Trust (MET) League of Colleges in Mumbai, India.

Not all my presentations on CA have been scholarly. In fact, many of the international presentations have occurred through invitations from business professionals, including advertising clubs, advertising agencies, chambers of commerce, designers of distance learning, software companies, and venture capitalists. They're all looking for ways to improve their creativity.

In the United States, I've presented CA at juried conferences that include the American Academy of Advertising Conference in St. Louis, Missouri; the Association of Educators in Journalism and Mass Communications Conferences in Washington DC, Miami Florida, and Boston Massachusetts; the National College Media Conference in St. Louis, Missouri; and the Broadcast Educators Association Conference in Las Vegas, Nevada.

But I've also been invited to present it to seven American Advertising Federations (AAF) in the 4th District (Florida and the Caribbean), including St. Thomas and St. Croix in the Virgin Islands. Also on the list are the Creative Club of San Antonio, Texas; the Houston, Texas office of Bates Advertising International; a Microsoft partner in Silicon Valley, California; a phone conglomerate in New England; and the New England Press Association in Boston, Massachusetts.

In addition, I've taught CA at universities in Massachusetts, Missouri, Texas, Florida, Illinois, and Rhode Island, and at the leading graduate institute of communications 7,000 miles away in India: Mudra Institute of Communications, Ahmedabad (MICA).

That's all well and good. But why have I gone into such detail about the acceptance of an ideation system you've probably never even heard of? For one important reason: CA is so different from the way most people access their creativity that you may be reluctant to try it. After all, how would you know that the process called CA will work for you?

Maybe this will give you some more brainfood for thought: I asked a well-respected colleague who has seen CA in presentations and in classrooms to give me her honest opinion about it, and this is what she said:

> I frequently asked Linda to lead creative sessions for my Copywriting and Advanced Creative Labs. Her methods of conceptualizing ideas produced amazing results from those who didn't consider themselves creative—as well as those who did. (Elaine L. Wagner, Professor Emerita, Advertising Department, College of Journalism and Communications, University of Florida)

Sitting in a classroom with a professor to explain things you don't understand, however, is very different from picking up this book and reading it by yourself. Of course, it would help to talk to my former students. Unfortunately, they're spread out all around the world, so it's somewhat difficult to locate them.

Here's something, though, that might relieve any doubts you may still have: they 'got' it (understood CA). How do I know this? Well, they captured more than 200 local, regional, national, and international advertising awards for their creativity, using CA: in the Creativity 39 International Student Awards; the Eighteenth Annual Summit International Creative Student Awards; the International Student Competition; the National Broadcast Competition Student Awards; the Missouri Broadcast Educators Association student competitions; and the American Advertising Federation's national, district, and local ADDY student competitions, the largest advertising competition in the United States.

Maybe you'd like to know more about my students. Many are American. They took classes with me at the University of North Texas; in Rhode Island School of Design's Certificate Program; at Northeastern University, Boston; Southeast Missouri State University; the University of Florida; and Southern Illinois University, Carbondale. But nearly one-third of them learned CA at MICA. And they have gone on to become successful writers, art directors, and creative directors globally, and at advertising agencies throughout India. You'll meet three of them in Chapter 18.

Creative Aerobics

From the start, I felt there was a need to find out whether CA was cross-cultural, or whether its use was limited to just the United States and to American culture. So I took it to a country with a very different culture but one that did business in English. Needless to say, when my MICA students received more than forty advertising awards from the listed student competitions, including Best of Show, my question was answered. In fact, the Director of the Crafting Creative Communications Programme at MICA made CA a required course. And for seven summers, I spent June and July in Ahmedabad, teaching it.

More recently, Dr Arpan Yagnik, my former student and now a coauthor of this book, introduced CA on the TEDx stage of The Pennsylvania State University, in Erie, where he is an Assistant Professor of advertising. Currently, he is teaching CA there in one of his advertising courses.

What are the specifics about CA that are likely to be important to you? You'll discover them in Chapter 1, which follows this Preface. And that should greatly increase your comfort level.

Arpan and I invite you on this journey. Happy reading and happy creating!

Acknowledgments

To the Mudra Institute of Communications, Ahmedabad (MICA) community who embraced Creative Aerobics (CA) when I taught there, and to those who contributed their insights when I asked for their thoughts: Sushil Bahl, a veteran advertising professional and academic who made my first article published in India, coauthored with him, a reality; Subhash Tendle, an advertising creative director-turned-Crafting-Creative-Communications-director who shared seven batches of his students with me and then let me share my students in southern Illinois with him; and Prasad Venkatraman, Elrid Carvalho, and Broty Ganguly, former students, now Indian advertising and communications superstars in their own rights. My deep appreciation to you all.

To the late Atul Tandan, then Director of MICA, who hired me and encouraged me to teach the discipline of CA to students, with award-winning results. May you rest in peace for centuries, Atul.

To my American and Indian students who worked so hard and so successfully to create the advertisements illustrated in this book. Thank you for letting me share them.

To Barbara Schweitzer who gave me the courage to see CA for what it is and can be. 'Thank you' is hardly sufficient.

To Dr John Sutherland, Head of the Advertising Department in the College of Journalism and Communications at the University of Florida, when I taught there, who recognized the value of CA in teaching students to write award-winning advertising. Much appreciated, John.

To Chapal Mehra, the editor of my first book, published by the Response Division of SAGE, who took a chance on the viability of CA. It worked!

To Manisha Mathews, the editor of this book, who has worked night, day, and on her own time to bring the subject to the world's attention. I'm so appreciative!

To Dr Arpan Yagnik, my coauthor and former student at MICA. Neither of us knew then that he'd be getting his PhD in the United States; that he'd be teaching/presenting CA at Penn State; and that we'd be writing this book together!

To my beloved daughter Shannon Conway Keith who has been there from the beginning, visiting my classes as a child; bracing me up when her loving stepfather Steve Correll died unexpectedly, and I turned to writing my first book to fill the huge void; and transitioning into her current role of a dear friend, a traveling companion, and a computer tech advisor. Hang in there, Shannie. There's one more to go.

Last but by no means least, to my husband of nearly six years, J.C. George. For years, he has been asking me to write a book about my life experiences, and I told him I had to finish this book first. It's done, J.C., and my next book's for you!

Linda Conway Correll George

First and foremost to Linda Ma'am for not giving up on me after the first day of the CA class, encouraging and supporting me in getting admitted to a doctoral program, and lastly for entrusting me with this invaluable honor and learning opportunity of sharing CA with the world.

Second, to all my teachers and mentors who played a vital role in empowering me with the abilities to express and contribute to society and to knowledge. I would like to especially mention Dr Srinivas Melkote, Dr Ashutosh Patel, and the late Zahida Chowdhary.

Third, my sisters for their continued selfless love and affection for me, which is something I consider myself extremely privileged to be a recipient of.

And last, to Manisha for being supportive, responsive, and prompt throughout this process.

Dr Arpan Yagnik

# Taking the Wraps/Raps off Creative Aerobics

The last week I was in residence at the Houston agency that I mentioned in the Preface, the creative director asked me if I would present Creative Aerobics (CA) to the copywriters and art directors in the creative department. I was delighted, and I did. It was an hour of fun-loving humor, a surprisingly large amount of participation, and deftly executed exercises and solutions. The enthusiasm for the process ran high.

After I finished the presentation, participants came up individually to thank me for showing them a way of coming up with ideas that they had never thought of before in approaching their assignments. They told me how valuable CA could be for them. And how much time they thought it could save. I couldn't have asked for a better response.

Here are some of the advantages they discovered:

1. Whether you work in advertising, interested in working in the field, or just want to sharpen and extend your creativity, you will have no trouble coming up with ideas. And you'll be able to come up with them in less than an hour. I call it creativity on demand. You'll find solutions as you step your way through the process. After you've completed the process, you'll go back and find a dozen or more solutions—in fact, at one of my international scholarly presentations, left-brained academic participants who didn't think of themselves as creative came up with more than 30 solutions in a 40-minute period. That included the time they spent learning the process and their time spent developing fresh, out-of-the-box ideas.

2. You will come up with ideas you never would have thought of, using your normal problem-solving skills. Generally, when I finish a session, I ask participants whether they would have arrived at the same solutions without CA. Nobody ever answers 'yes'.
3. You will come up with multiple ideas in less than an hour, maybe even more quickly.
4. You will enjoy coming up with ideas. It will feel like play. There's no anxiety. No panic. Just relaxing, laughter-induced creative thinking, and results.
5. Each CA exercise is designed to encourage your readers/customers to read every word you wrote. (It is estimated that 90 percent of people noting ads will read only the headline, missing the message/sell). How?

    In Creative Aerobics 1, you're finding little-known facts about your product and adding a twist. The twist creates an individual point of view that entices the reader into the copy. It can be either verbal or visual.

    In Creative Aerobics 2, you're creating new what-it-isn't names for your product, and the reader must delve into the copy to figure out the connections.

    In Creative Aerobics 3, you're expressing the relationship between new 'names' and your product, and identifying the similarities between them in your copy.

    In Creative Aerobics 4, you're creating new definitions for existing phrases that force your reader to view the product from a different perspective, spelling out the differences in the copy.
6. This may be the most important reason of all for learning CA. The process will become **you**. Not the other way around. Think of it in the context of American football, where team members have to learn a playbook. The more they practice the plays, the more the plays become a part of their performance on the field—or in your case, the creative field. You both can own them.

Creative Aerobics

You'll find that the more you use CA, the more proficient you will become. Soon, it will be second nature—when you start an assignment, you will automatically turn to CA. Think of it as **you**, coming up with fresh, interesting, in-your-face ideas to capture people's attention and interest—**and always keep in mind that there are more than three billion, and counting, users of the Internet besides you, who can be exposed to the same information you are for their ideas, and who may be competing against you!**

What is going to make your CA ideas fresh/interesting/impactful/ effective is that they present your product or idea differently from the way readers are used to experience it. And in ways that force readers to 'get it'—the individual point of view, the new name, the similarities between dissimilars, and the new definition. 'Getting it', after all, is kind of like the punchline of a joke—it rewards you for listening/reading.

Actually, that isn't too far off the mark, especially with CA4. 'Getting it'—the new definition for the existing phrase—often provides a little humor, which works to your advantage in raising the likeability of your advertising/writing. And if people like what you're writing, it can increase reader interest in your product/idea.

Are you ready now to discover how CA can improve your creativity? If you are, let's start with some brain warm-up exercises. I've placed them at the end of this chapter and the next four chapters, so that you can begin to build your left and right brain flexibility. Please complete them as you go, so you'll be prepared for the CA exercises when you get to them.

P.S. It is very okay to write in your book!

Exercise 1: Words, Words, Words

This is an exercise you're probably familiar with: rearranging the letters in a word to form other words. So take the word 'advertisement', and see if you can find fifty four-letter-or-more words. Avoid proper names such as Sean, Ivan, or Vera. Avoid foreign words (*vert*, the French word for green', for example). Avoid slang and abbreviations. Use the root of a word only **once** ('Dart', Not 'dart'; 'darts', and 'darted').

For your information, there are more than 200 words you can find!

1.	14.	27.	40.
2.	15.	28.	41.
3.	16.	29.	42.
4.	17.	30.	43.
5.	18.	31.	44.
6.	19.	32.	45.
7.	20.	33.	46.
8.	21.	34.	47.
9.	22.	35.	48.
10.	23.	36.	49.
11.	24.	37.	50.
12.	25.	38.	
13.	26.	39.	

Were you able to find fifty words? Good job! Now, stretch your thinking cap a little further.

 **Brainwork**

Here's a question you probably haven't been asked before: What did your brain feel like when you were doing this exercise? You were given everything you needed to complete the assignment— thirteen letters, two of which appeared more than once (three 'e's and two 't's). You had three vowels and seven consonants to work with. Also, it is likely that you had done a similar exercise at some time in the past, which avoided the stress of learning a new thought process—that must have provided a level of comfort for you. How did you proceed? Once you formed a word, did you go back and find additional words by substituting each of the remaining consonants for the first letter of your formed word (dart = tart, mart, start)? How many additional words did that make? How long did it take you to complete this task? Summing the experience up, would you label this a straightforward left-brained experience? Or did a little right-brained thinking sneak in when you were substituting the consonants?

Exercise 2

Find twenty words that contain the consonants T, R, B, and L. You must use all selected letters in each word. And you must follow the guidelines in Exercise 1 as to what is acceptable and what is not.

1.	6.	11.	16.
2.	7.	12.	17.
3.	8.	13.	18.
4.	9.	14.	19.
5.	10.	15.	20.

How does your brain feel now? There's a level of comfort in having a framework in which to think. But now your brain is asking, "Should I start the words with one of the consonants, or …?" "Should I use two of the consonants together, or …"

When your brain begins asking questions and adding internal answers to the exercise, the parameters of your thought process stretch. "Yes, I'll start with two consonants together," you decide. And you come up with **trouble**. **Blotter.**

"What happens if I separate the consonants," you wonder: **Laboratory**.

"Suppose I start with a vowel or a different consonant." **Irritable**. **Stumbler**.

Notice what is happening to your thinking as you add more internal answers. Are the answers coming faster? Are you finding more questions as you go? Does finding ten words with the given criteria seem doable? What about finding fifty words?

Your brain should be feeling tired now. But the fatigue should be accompanied by a sense of accomplishment. You met the criteria. Congratulations!

Exercise 3

Are you ready to pick out your own three or four consonants, and create your own rules?

Create your rules and write them here (Don't forget to jot down your four letters):

_____

_____

Now, follow your rules and find twenty words that meet your criteria:

1.	6.	11.	16.
2.	7.	12.	17.
3.	8.	13.	18.
4.	9.	14.	19.
5.	10.	15.	20.

Go ahead and take a break. Get a snack. Get something to drink. Or get both! I used to encourage my students to be sure and eat something before they came to class. It's not easy to create on an empty stomach.

Creative Aerobics

 ## In the Beginning ...

As a professor at the University of Florida, I used to start the first class of every copywriting and visualization course with the following introduction:

Let me tell you about myself. In the middle of my freshman year at one of the most rigorous private colleges in the country, my English Literature professor called me in to review my work. "In my 12 years of college teaching," she began, "You are the first student who has failed to get the point of my course."

FAILED???

Why would I admit failure to my students? After all, I went on to make my living as a copywriter, VP/group head, and VP/creative director for 31 years in advertising agencies from Madison Avenue, New York to the largest cities in Texas. I won more than fifty awards from regional, national, and international advertising competitions such as the New York Festivals, the Telly Awards, the Clio Awards, the Summit Awards, the Annual Creativity Awards, and the ADDY Awards. And I did it using an unorthodox approach I had arrived at through trial and error—an alternative thinking process employing both the left and right brains that I would eventually develop into a system I called 'Creative Aerobics'. But until I began using CA, I always worried as I approached an assignment whether, despite my experience and awards, I would be able to come up with fresh, creative ideas.

Sidebar 1

The Left and Right Brains

Nobel Prize winner Roger Sperry won the Prize "for his work on what is commonly known as right brain-left brain thinking. Sperry theorized that some very specific activities were controlled by one side of the human brain or the other—for example, the right side controlled creative tasks, while the left side was where logic, language and reasoning lived."[1]

Back to the classroom. I knew that having to learn an unconventional process like CA and to use it for an entire semester would strip away my students' self-confidence and preconceived ideas of how to write effective, creative advertising; it would force them to follow a predetermined route through a series of specific word exercises they may not have learned before. They would experience frustration. Failure. And it would take them at least a month to become comfortable and to begin achieving success using this system.

What was wrong with their current creative thought process, anyway? You've probably used it yourself. See if this sounds familiar:

You're given an assignment or a problem to solve, so,

Step 1. The first thing you do is to become totally familiar with the assignment. You collect background information on the product or problem. How much and what type of information depends on your previous experience in collecting it.

One of the problems I ran into with students was they didn't collect ENOUGH information, or they didn't collect information they could work with. So the collection experience itself was as important as what they found.

---

[1] Retrieved on January 5, 2014, from www/dyslexiavictoriaonline.com

Step 2. You absorb the information you've collected. And discuss it with the members of your team if it's a group project.

Step 3. Now you let the information percolate. Ideas may come immediately. Or they may arrive at a time when you're concentrating on something else. There's no way to tell.

Step 4. You get the group together and share your ideas with them; you listen to the ideas they've come up with. Or maybe you brainstorm together, although in the past you've found that to be uncomfortable. After you've shared ideas, you evaluate them, deciding which best meet(s) the assignment criteria.

Sound about right? Well, what's the time frame for **your** system? A morning? A day? A week?

And that's the problem: you can't determine how much time it's going to take to arrive at the solution. Ironically, you've had facts, facts, and more facts at your fingertips almost from the start of your search. Thank the Information Age and your speedy research assistants Google and Bing for that!

But with faster access to information comes this century's expectation of shorter deadlines and quicker solutions. That increases stress and burnout—two of creativity's biggest enemies.

What if your information base could generate creative solutions **as** it was being gathered, rather than **after** collection? And what if it could generate **multiple creative solutions**? In other words, you'd be arriving at your answers while you were still working the exercises.

I believe that Creativity on Demand can, and that it does, happen.

Hmm. Maybe from this point forward, you should consider changing **your** ideation model to mine.

Are you willing to put **yourself** and your creativity to the test? Think about it for a moment. There's risk involved. That's always uncomfortable. But creativity is not a spectator sport. You need to tackle everything directly, whether you're working by yourself, or whether you decide to put a group of friends together to work on the CA exercises.

Whoa! We're getting ahead of ourselves. That can wait until Chapter 7. You have some more warm-up territory to cover!

Exercise 4: Forward and Backward

Find fifty three-letter-or-more words that, when spelled backwards, form a *new* word: (for example: ton = not). Avoid proper names, foreign words, slang, and abbreviations. Plural forms of words are fine (for example: rat = tar, rats = star).

1.	14.	27.	40.
2.	15.	28.	41.
3.	16.	29.	42.
4.	17.	30.	43.
5.	18.	31.	44.
6.	19.	32.	45.
7.	20.	33.	46.
8.	21.	34.	47.
9.	22.	35.	48.
10.	23.	36.	49.
11.	24.	37.	50.
12.	25.	38.	
13.	26.	39.	

 **Brainwork**

Exercise 2 gives you parameters but no guidelines. How are you going to get started? Twirl random words around in your head? That's certainly an option, though an inefficient one. Before you go there, go here: to the first two paragraphs of this chapter.

 Creative Aerobics

The third word in paragraph one is the three-letter word 'was'. **backwards**, it spells 'saw'. And in paragraph two, you'll find 'are', which, when reversed, yields 'era'.

One tactic you can use is to go through this book, tracking down reversible three-letter words. Another strategy is one that you used in Exercise 1—replacing the first letter of the word with a different consonant—'s' changed to 'r', and 'saw' becomes 'raw', which, spelled backwards, becomes 'war'.

Before leaving this example, try changing the first consonant in 'war' to a 'g'. 'War' becomes 'gar', a species of fish, which backwards becomes 'rag'. Change the 'g' to an 'm' and 'gar' becomes 'mar', which backwards is 'ram'. Change the 'm' to a 'p'—'par', and it reverses to 'rap'. A change of the 'p' to 't' in 'par' becomes 'tar/rat'; a change of the 'r' in 'rap' to a 't' becomes 'tap/pat'.

A third option is to change the vowel. Take the last pair 'tap/pat'. An 'i' will change it to 'tip/pit'. An 'o' will result in 'top/pot'. And a fourth option is to pluralize: 'tap' becomes 'taps/spat'; 'top' becomes 'tops/spot'; and 'pot' becomes 'pots/stop'.

 **Brainstretch**

When you were first asked to find fifty words that could be reversed to form a different word, how did your brain respond? Was there a feeling of being overwhelmed and at loose ends? Messy thinking, perhaps? How does it feel now? You've found eleven pairs: war/raw, gar/rag, mar/ram, par/rap, tar/rat, tap/pat, tip/pit, top/pot, taps/spat, tops/spot, and pots/stop. Pluralize words in some of the other pairs you've found, and you can increase the number: raps/spar, rats/star, and tips/spit.

Again, you've been able to mix your left-brained thinking—the word/reversal process—with your right-brained thinking—the random letter/substitution process.

Exercise 5

Can you feel how sharp and focused your thinking is after doing the exercise? Go back to your fifty pairs above, and see if you can select ten pairs that you can add an 's' to, to form additional pairs.

1. 5. 9.
2. 6. 10.
3. 7.
4. 8.

The more exercises you complete, the better you're preparing yourself to begin learning CA.

Why not start on CA now? You have five exercises behind you.

Because you still need to establish context for what you're doing—a frame of reference.

Because you need to be working with ideas, not just techniques.

Because you need to learn how to define creativity for yourself.

Because you still need to work more on building your left-brain/right-brain flexibility and coordination.

Because we're sending a mental moving van/lorry to your brain and transporting it to an unfamiliar location.

Because we don't want you to get lost along the way!

David versus Goliath, AKA Small versus The Big Idea

I was still working in advertising—at the time, for an agency in Dallas, Texas that had multiple offices across the country—when I heard this story about one of my former colleagues. He had been promoted to creative director of the agency's West Coast office.

The president of the company had invited creative directors from all the offices to join him for dinner; and after dinner, he asked them to present an overview of the work being done by each office.

One after another, they got up and made their presentations. Soon, attendees began to yawn. Heads nodded. Eyes closed. Until my friend—let's call him Harry—rose.

Harry dragged his chair over to the head of the table, climbed up on the chair, and stepped onto the dinner table.

Now, all eyes and attention were focused on Harry.

He began singing his presentation. And at the same time, he started tap dancing down the table, kicking dirty cups, plates and silverware onto the floor, and into the laps of his fellow creative directors.

Nobody ever forgot Harry's presentation.

It was a Big Idea! It broke through the ordinary, run-of-the-mill reports and changed perception. It turned presentation styles upside down. It was talked about for years!

As you may expect, Harry's Big Idea got him fired. Which is not to say Big Ideas are bad. In fact, one expectation of creativity is that it will produce new ideas and/or Big Ideas.

If you google 'The Big Idea', you may be surprised to learn that there are more than 1 billion references to this phrase around the world, but I'll mention just a few, to show the variety of its application. The entries include video games and board games, a band, a television show called The Big Idea, church ministries, New Zealand's creative community, and a monthly column in the British newspaper, *The Guardian*.

But wait. There's more.

The term 'The Big Idea' actually goes back a number of years. It was the title of a 1917 black and white silent film starring comedian Harold Lloyd. More recently, New Orleans called its 2013 Entrepreneur Week, 'The Big Idea event'. Pittsburgh has its friendly neighborhood radical Big Idea bookstore and café. Even the *Harvard Business Review* in its March 2010 issue carried an article titled 'The Big Idea: Finding Eureka'.

New England agency's principal Edward Boches addressed the Big Idea in his November 19, 2013, blog: "You could argue that big ideas still work—if you define a big idea as something that becomes part of the cultural landscape, generates awareness and conversation among many, endures the test of time (or at least dominates the moment), and needs traditional media or advertising to call attention to it."

On the other hand, if you go back to George Lois' (Advertising Hall of Fame member, art director, and agency principal) criteria that it has to *change* popular culture (rather than reflect it), transform our language, launch a new business or idea, and 'turn the world upside down'—well, that's another story.

No matter which definition you prefer, Big Ideas don't come along every day. But when they do, they can produce a dramatic rise in sales/results, as well as a stronger relationship with your client/customer.

Let's take a look at the 'Dirt is Good' advertising campaign for international Unilever Company's laundry detergent OMO, and for Hindustan Unilever's product Surf Excel. Three years ago, the company initiated a global survey of 12,000 parents in ten countries to learn more about the play habits of the parents' children, ages seven to twelve. What the results of the research showed was a decline in outdoor play among these kids, in favor of playing games inside on their computers. In fact, eight out of ten parents said their kids often refused to play unless there was some form of technology involved. It was going to take a Big Idea to make them desert their computers and move outdoors again.

The company shared this information with its advertising agency, MullenLowe Advertising, Singapore and charged it with developing a campaign that would reverse this trend.

A three-time world champion sand sculptor, Joo Heng Tan, was hired and instructed to **physically build** three huge 18-ton sculptures for kids to play in. That's a lot of sand! (At two inches deep, it's about 180 square meters per sculpture).

One of the sculptures recreated the surface of the moon, complete with a rocket and craters.

While parents might be leery—dirt is the enemy, after all—was there a kid on earth who could resist an extraterrestrial moon crater landscape, complete with the skeleton of a dinosaur inside the crater, as a playground? It was a Big Idea!

It goes without saying that the kids loved it. But what about their parents? What was their 'take' on this? Surprisingly, they began looking at 'dirt' differently. Now it was a good thing, aiding in their children's development.

The ultimate measure of the success of the campaign, however, was expressed on the bottom line. Sales increased nearly 1,000 times over! Sales grew from approximately US$4.73 million to about US$3.7 billion.[1]

I can't tell you how many times during my career in advertising I heard the words, "What we need now is a Big Idea." It came from management, account executives, researchers, and even creative directors, who should have known better.

In my experience, Big Ideas start out as those fresh, small, out-of-the-box thoughts CA generates for you. And then they grow

---

[1] Retrieved from www.adweek.com/news/advertising-branding/unilevers-true-g

up! It is so much more productive—and less time consuming, by the way—to keep adding on elements and dimensions until your thoughts scream "I'm a Big Idea now!"

Let me explain that with a campaign I did for a regional Doors and Windows Company in New England. The company was expanding its marketing territory, moving into a region with established competition. The company's and its competitor's product lines were similar, although our client's lines were priced slightly below competition's. Also, our client had a weapon that the competition didn't have: computerized inventory and order taking. While it was taking competition a week to fill and ship orders, our client could fill them, load pallets, and turn orders all in a single day. But we knew it would be a tough sell to pry building supply customers away from their existing trade relationships with our client's competitor.

We addressed the problem head-on: we asked our competition's customers to 'Bite the Bullet' and make the tough decision to switch their business to our client. And we made the request in a big way: with our advertising.

Our media department reserved four-color, double-page spreads in regional editions of the leading building trade publications that our prospective customers read. They had observed that the majority of the ads in these publications were less than a page in size, and used limited color, if any at all. That told us that the two-page ads and the use of full color would have enormous impact on readers, as would the position where we planned to place them: the magazines' centerfolds.

The visual in the introductory ad was striking: an immense golden, metallic bullet that stretched across the two pages. No one had ever seen a bullet used as the visual for a Doors and Windows Company advertisement before, never mind a bullet that large. We chose the bullet visual for several reasons: for impact, obviously. And for speed: bullets can travel 2,500 feet a second—nearly a half mile; and some, upwards of 1,200 meters a second. Also, bullets do have a reputation for hitting their targets.

Creative Aerobics

In essence, then, we were telling a new audience that our client could make faster, more accurate order deliveries to them. But we also used the bullet for the demographics and psychographics of our target audience. Our potential customers were located in a predominantly male customer base; and the majority of them were gun owners who looked forward to the hunting season every year. The bullet ad would catch their eye.

The ad ran the month prior to the annual building trades show, alerting these potential customers to visit our client's booth at the show. In addition to printing extra copies of the ad for handouts, we also had chocolate bullets made and wrapped in shiny gold paper. They were attached to a handsome invitation that encouraged recipients to visit our client's hospitality suite, and included the message 'Bite the Bullet'. In other words, this time it meant "Come and enjoy refreshments with us." At the show's booth, employees handed out reprints of the ad, along with the invitation, which directed traffic to the Suite. It was the talk of the show, and our client picked up a sizable amount of business from it.

Could we have expanded our Big Idea? As I think of it now, and if the budget had allowed, we might have turned large, empty bullet shells/casings into key rings engraved with the company's name, phone number, website address, and variation of our message: "I Bit the Bullet." The key rings would be handed out to trade show attendees who 'bit' and visited the hospitality suite. Once taken back home to attendees' places of business, these leave-behinds could become conversation starters, raising interest about what our client had to offer among fellow employees who didn't attend the show.

Going further, we might have expanded our sphere of influence, and approached new business prospects at noncompeting companies, sharing the success story behind our 'Bite the Bullet' campaign with them—how it had hit the mark in attracting new customers for our Doors and Windows client.

We could have initiated contact with a 'teaser' mailing to their key players—the president, the advertising director, etc. Maybe it would be a (slightly crumpled) used paper bull's-eye target with a single bullet hole in the bull's-eye, a little off-center. The headline might read, "We'd like a shot at showing you what our advertising programs can do for clients."

The agency logo might be printed on the back of the piece. Or it might be a 'blind' mailing.

A week later, we'd follow it up with a second mailing: an attention-getting, round-shaped brochure that replicated the bull's-eye shooting target; printing the concentric circles on it that measured a shooter's accuracy; punching 'bullet hole(s)' through the center of the bull's-eye, and maybe through the whole brochure (screening the bull's-eye at a 15 percent concentration on each page as a mnemonic to reinforce our story), to communicate that our work is accurate and on target; and giving a detailed history and results story of the campaign inside.

The third week, we would follow up with a phone call to the company's advertising manager to schedule a new business presentation meeting.

Future new business presentations would give us an opportunity to amortize the production costs of the bullet-casing key rings idea described above, since the key rings could gain additional mileage as leave-behinds and conversation starters following those presentations.

Whew!

It proves once again that the advantage of thinking small is the depth to which your creativity can descend. And the breadth of attention-grabbing ideas that it can summon up!

Sidebar 2

Measuring the Dimensions of a Big Idea

If you're attempting to create a Big Idea, it's helpful to have a measuring stick to evaluate it, after the brainstorming, of course. **Never**

evaluate during a creativity session. Wait until after it—criticism shuts down creativity. Here's a list of criteria that provides a good rule of thumb:

- "Big Ideas must **resonate** with consumers." "Dirt is Good" resonates. It addresses the inherent tension between moms' controlling desire to keep their children from getting dirty, and their realization that getting dirty has benefits. The idea is relatively simple. But it is provocative. And although it is rational, a Big Idea also usually has an emotional component.[2]
- "Big Ideas are disruptive."[3] They're game changers. They can turn convention on its head. In extreme cases, they represent a new way of thinking, feeling, or acting. Expanding the landscape, from a backyard sandbox to an 18-ton sand behemoth, is a new way of thinking about 'Dirt'.
- "Big Ideas have talk value."[4] They're water cooler topics of conversation, where proponents discuss their reactions to these emotionally charged, highly resonant, game-changing propositions.
- "Big Ideas stretch brands."[5] Unilever flew 250 of its marketing executives of varying ethnicities and nationalities to Cape Town, South Africa to get filthy as members of a work gang. It was the only way its Global Brand Vice President believed the company's far-flung family would buy into 'Dirt is a good thing'.[6]

---

[2] Retrieved on January 8, 2014, from www.millwardbrown.com/libraries/MB_pov_D

[3] Ibid.

[4] Ibid.

[5] Ibid.

[6] Retrieved on January 14, 2014, from www.adweek.com/news/advertising-branding/unilevers-true-g

- "Big Ideas transcend cultural and geographic boundaries."[7] They are truly universal, cutting across class, gender, age, and ethnicity to communicate at a fundamental human level. 'Dirt is Good' really wasn't a cleaning message. It was a social message. When it was tested in Brazil, the results were positive, leading Unilever to contemplate introducing the message to Latin America, Europe, and much of Asia. Was the campaign successful? Sales grew from approximately US$4.73 million to about US$3.7 billion.[8]

If you're wondering why I introduced this chapter so early in the book, there's a reason: I'm dangling a 'carrot'—make that a 14-karat idea—in front of you. It's to let you know the exciting kinds of things you can think up, once you have CA under your belt.

Exercise 6: Four for Four

Here is the next of the warm-up exercises. It asks you to turn 25 four-letter words into 100 words. And here's how you'll do it:

1. Select a four-letter word.
2. Now change the **second** letter of your word to form additional words. If your second letter is a vowel, substitute each of the vowels. If your second letter is a consonant, substitute each of the consonants.
3. When you've exhausted all your choices, go back to your **original** word and change the **third** letter of your word to form additional words. Substitute each letter of the alphabet for it.

---

[7] See www.millwardbrown.com/libraries/MB
[8] See www.adweek.com/news/advertising-branding/unilevers-true-g

4. Total the number of words you've found; it must produce a minimum of four additional words.
5. Be sure you don't change both letters at the same time.

We've selected the word 'date' for you to work with. Since 'a' is the second letter—a vowel—run the four remaining vowels. Changing the 'a' to 'e' results in 'dete'. It's not a word. Changing the 'a' to 'i' results in 'dite' which is not an English word, although it appears in Latin. Changing the 'a' to 'o' produces 'dote', a verb that means 'to shower with love'. Changing the 'a' to 'u'—'dute'—no. The second letter change gave you a total of one additional word.

Ready to change letter three? It's a consonant—'t'. Run through the alphabet: 'l' gives you 'dale'; 'm' gives you 'dame'; 'r' gives you 'dare'. The third letter change produced three additional words giving you a total of four words. Your answer would look like this:

> date
> dote
> dale
> dame
> dare

Words with vowels as the second and fourth letters, which is the case in 'date', work well. Let's try another combination: one vowel and three consonants: 'part', for example. Changing the second letter, a vowel, will give us 'pert' and 'port'. Running the alphabet for the third letter change produces 'pact' and 'pant', giving you the requisite four additional words:

> part
> pert
> port
> pact
> pant

Now, it's your turn.

1.	6.	11.	16.	21.
2.	7.	12.	17.	22.
3.	8.	13.	18.	23.
4.	9.	14.	19.	24.
5.	10.	15.	20.	25.

Exercise 7

This is your opportunity to see what happens when you apply the four-for-four rule to your derivatives above. But apply it with a twist: take the first derivative of a first derivative. In other words, 'dame' is a first derivative of 'date' (you also could have chosen dote, dale, or dare). Run vowels through 'dame' to find a first derivative of it: 'dime', for example. We'll work with 'dime'. A first derivative of it is 'dame', of course. And 'dome'. Now, let's run the consonants. And we find dice, dike, dine, dire, and dive.

Pick ten of your four-for-four solutions above. Follow the directions for finding your first derivative's derivatives (it just sounds complicated). Got it?

1.
2.
3.
4.
5.

6.
7.
8.
9.
10.

Creative Aerobics

Exercise 8

Here's another way to work with four-letter words. Select ten words, which allow you to rearrange the letters to form two additional words. For example, **meat**/mate/tame(/team).

1.   5.   9.
2.   6.   10.
3.   7.
4.   8.

Defining the Creative Process Today

In Chapter 2, we took a brief look at an ideation system that's been used for years by professional thinkers, writers, poets, artists, marketers, and anybody trying to come up with an idea. I'd like to revisit it, look at a couple of other ideation techniques, and identify how CA differs noticeably from them, and why it may serve you better in today's creative climate.

The four stages of the creative process—preparation, incubation, illumination, and verification—were identified in 1926 by Graham Wallas, the cofounder of the London School of Economics. It became the go-to model for arriving at ideas.

Thirteen years later, in 1939, James Webb Young, a vice president at J. Walter Thompson (JWT) advertising agency in New York City, addressed the creative process in his 48-page book *A Technique for Producing Ideas*. It listed five steps in the process: immersion, digestion, incubation, illumination, and reality/verification.

Both of these men proposed techniques that stepped you through the process a step at a time, progressing from one stage to another; in other words, they used linear thinking.

In 1967, Dr Edward de Bono introduced another way of thinking creatively, which he called 'lateral thinking'. It differed from linear or vertical, thinking by employing alternatives, non-sequential, undoing of selection processes, and a shift in attention or focus—nontraditional ways of examining a task.

The year 1974 saw Tony Buzan add a new phrase to the creative process vocabulary—'mind mapping', a graphic technique he developed that uses an image/picture for the central idea; colored pencils to illustrate the diagram; and curved branches for second- and third-level associations.

What strikes me about each of these ideation techniques is that there's something missing from them: they lack interrelationship among their individual steps—simplification; and they lack time streaming—a way to save time and speed the process along. Today, we need a simpler, faster way to search out ideas.

Faster and simpler: those are two of the missing links that CA can supply. Since the CA exercises are related to each other, they're step savers. And since they *immediately* begin to build solutions/relationships/connections as you perform them, they're time savers. You may start to recognize results while you're in the process of implementing an exercise. Or you may not recognize your solutions until you complete all four exercises and review your results. It really doesn't matter: after you've practiced CA for a short period of time, you'll begin to relax and enjoy the process, knowing your project is in good hands—yours.

Why do I say that?

Because the exercises are very specific in focus. They are always the same. (Do you realize what a comfort level that provides?) They are capable of building an enormous database of information. And it's a database that's completely open-ended, depending upon the number of pieces of information you choose to work with.

I feel comfortable in saying that, when you finish the four exercises, the solutions will be in place. In fact, there will be multiple solutions. And your ideation work will be done.

Really?????

At this moment, you may be questioning my sanity! I would be, too, if I hadn't watched CA in action for 26 years. And if I hadn't seen a student, who'd told me she was too left-brained to do anything creative, win Best of Show in the Student American Advertising Federations (AAF) ADDY Awards competition the month after she finished my class. She did it with a campaign I would never have thought of—one that was uniquely her own!

This, I think, is the real value of CA: it is authentic. Your CA experience will be very different from mine. And very different from the experiences of the thousands of students I've taught.

It will allow you to reach down into the depths of your creativity and arrive at solutions that will be individually yours. Your ideas will be shaped by the person you are, and by the experiences you've had. Even though you may access information available to everyone who visits the Internet—all three billion-and-counting of them—the results of how you work with the information you find will be *sui generis* (this is a Latin phrase meaning 'unique' or 'one of a kind, like no other'. I came across it in a conference meeting with my peers at the second agency I worked for. Not being one of the sophisticated, savvy New Yorkers they were, I thought, in my naiveté, they were talking about 'Suey generous'—large bowls of Chinese food!).

And that's the third advantage of using CA—you are unlikely to produce work that is a copy of other peoples' thinking. You will be surrounded by your original ideas. Your individual creativity will come shining through! (Who knows? It might even become a Big Idea!)

In light of this discussion about the creative process, have you given any thought to how you would define 'creativity?' Is it a new solution to a problem? Is it the ability to produce something new through imagination or a person's skills? Is creativity the ability to view things in new ways or from different perspectives? Is it making new connections or associations you haven't made before? Or...

My daughter produced her own definition of creativity and put it to work when she was eight years old. Once a week, I would ask her to pick up her room. Shannon **hated** cleaning her room. So she made the connection that if she took panels of fabric she had left over from crafts projects and draped them artfully over each messy spot—changing the room's appearance and my perception of it—she could give me the impression she'd picked up. Although she hadn't cleaned her room, she'd found a new solution to cleaning it—creativity in action.

My definition of creativity, like CA, is process driven: "looking through a magnifying glass into a kaleidoscope."

I like to begin my thinking with an extreme close up (ECU)—zooming in to examine every nook and cranny of inspiration in extreme detail; going bigger than life, looking for shape and texture, variations, and idiosyncrasies that set my field of vision apart.

I project my field of vision through a mind cylinder that houses the mirrors and colors, patterns, and reflections of distortion and manipulation, observing how they reshape and polish my thinking into a freshly delivered idea.

Creativity for me is usually a push–pull process. Once you reach the chapters that outline exercises for each Creative Aerobic, you'll discover it, too: you'll begin to see how CA breaks down the creative process into steps, then builds it up into ideas.

Speaking of ideas, ponder this: the exercises you've been completing at the end of each chapter have been reducing language to its lowest common denominator: the **letters** that make up, or that change **words**. They're abstract verbal warm-ups that will stretch your left and right brains, making them more flexible. You'll begin to look at words in a different, narrower context, stripping away your normal interaction with them. Yet, each exercise is open-ended, so there isn't the stress of having to come up with the right answer; there are many right answers. And after all, you're going to need **words** to express your **ideas!**

Here's your next exercise:

Exercise 9: Two for One

In this exercise, you'll work your brain in a different way. Rather than rearranging letters, you'll work with finding pairs of words: fifty pairs of homophones—words that **sound** same, but are spelled differently (Note: there are three homophones in the title of this exercise: two/to/too, for/four/fore, and one/won). There are no caveats here—you can use proper names, slang, and foreign words. Just make sure that the vowel sound is the same. For example, pear = pare = pére (French for father). **Not** ferry/fairy.

You may be tempted to visit your computer and google 'homophones'. Please don't. You'll miss the endorphins and feelings of elation/discovery that are released every time you find one.

1.	14.	27.	40.
2.	15.	28.	41.
3.	16.	29.	42.
4.	17.	30.	43.
5.	18.	31.	44.
6.	19.	32.	45.
7.	20.	33.	46.
8.	21.	34.	47.
9.	22.	35.	48.
10.	23.	36.	49.
11.	24.	37.	50.
12.	25.	38.	
13.	26.	39.	

 **Brainwork**

Well, if you don't google your homophones, how are you going to find them? Here's a thought: look at your computer keyboard. You'll find at least two (lock = loch; pause = paws).

Where else can you look? At any printed material or Web page. For example, the front page of a Nashville, Tennessee, newspaper gave up: in (inn); where (wear, ware); phase (Fay's); new (knew, gnu); to (two, too); meet (meat); for (four); road (rode); won (one); some (sum); law (lore); Maine (main, mane); gym (Jim); whether (weather); hour (our); team (teem); shoe (shoo); counsel (council); led (lead); fair (fare)—twenty homophones.[1]

 **Brainstretch**

Here's another tool you can use with homophones. Often, you'll find them hiding in words that rhyme with the ones you've already found. So return to the newspaper homophone 'where/wear/ware'. Its rhymes yield air (heir); bear (bare); fair (fare), as noted above; flare (flair); hair (hare); pare (pear etc.), which have already been discussed; stare (stair); tear (tare).

Sometimes, you can add another letter to your homophone or your rhyme to find an additional pair: hair + y = hairy (Harry); Sin + e = Sine (sign); and Win + e = Wine (whine).

Exercise 10

See if you can think of any other word tools (tulles) you can use, and jot them down. You can try alternates to the ones I've outlined or create your own.

For example, start at the beginning of the alphabet and see how many double letter-together words you can find: AArdvark, buBBle, suCCess, etc.

---

[1] See *The Tennessean*. January 6, 2014.

Or beginning with 'ab', put together adjoining letters and search for words containing them: ABout, DEciDE, EFfort, etc._____

_____
_____
_____
_____
_____
_____
_____

 Developing Your Creative Magnifying Glass

In the last chapter, I spoke about the magnifying glass that lets me examine my creativity in more detail. Let's see what words speak to you when you peer into the virtual microscope of your imagination.

Mentally, pick a pink floribunda blossom (aka rose). How many petals are there in the rose? If you google it, you'll discover that there can be from five to fifty petals in a blossom, depending on the size and species of the flower. Your rose has forty to fifty petals. It's an approximate answer. At least, it gives us a frame of reference, sort of.

Secondary research—two-dimensional information that has already been disseminated—is useful in providing general answers to specific questions. What it omits, however, is the actual three-dimensional experience with the rose.

Primary research—direct contact with what you are studying—allows you to use your other senses, in addition to the sense of sight, to dig beneath the surface for answers. With a rose in hand, you can count its specific number of petals. You can inhale its scent—is it sweet? Woodsy? Perfume-y? What other adjectives come to mind? You can touch its petals—are they soft? Velvety? Moist? If you crumple them between your fingers, do they make a sound? A flutter? A whisper? And if you were to taste them, what would the sensation be?

My grandmother used to pick and dry rose petals, which she sprinkled with cinnamon. She would store them in an airtight container until they looked like deeply tanned cornflakes; and when they had reached a spicy sweetness, she would transfer them to an imported fine china jar with a gold-ringed top, where they would reside, like summer potpourri. On visits to her, my sister and I were allowed to sniff their intoxicating fragrance. It's a scent I can still recreate in my mind.

What about you? What scents can you remember in detail? And what about touch—do you recall the cool, smooth, metallic feel of the handle bars of your first bicycle? The more deeply you can dig into the subject you're exploring, using all of your senses, the more relevant and insightful the information that is revealed.

What does this have to do with today's business world? And why is it important?

According to an article in the *McKinsey Quarterly*, a 50-year-old business magazine that focuses on management and organization theory, there is a dark side to the Information Age: "information overload(,) and its close cousin, attention fragmentation .... One might think that constant exposure to new information ... makes us more creative .... Unfortunately, current research indicates the opposite .... Always-on, multi-tasking work environments are killing productivity, dampening creativity, and making us unhappy."[1]

In theory, each of us is surrounded by not only information overload, but by the **identical** information overload. When you google 'number of petals in a rose', you most likely will come up with the same references I did. The gnawing question is this: In a world where everyone can access the same content, how do we go about developing an individual identity for what we create? It's growing more and more important in every endeavor, especially business.

That's what this book is about.

---

[1] Dean, Derek and Caroline Webb (2011). "Recovering from Information Overload" *McKinsey Quarterly*, January. Retrieved June 21, 2017 from http://www.mckinsey.com/business-functions/organization/our-insights/recovering-from-information-overload

Creative Aerobics

Welcome to Your New Address: Madison Avenue[2]

Pack up your ideas. You're going to be moving your thinking to a new place—advertising.

Why advertising?

1. Because it is all about selling: selling ideas, selling products, selling services, selling individual points of view, even selling your kids on the idea that it's time to go to bed. Selling is a negotiation we do 24/7. And finding fresh, persuasive, and unusual ways to do it is a skill set highly sought after by the 21st century global business community.

Why advertising?

2. Because it will be a short learning curve for you. Without knowing it, you already know advertising like the back of your mind. How many television commercials have you watched in your lifetime? If you started watching TV as a child, you probably became aware of them when you were, say, six years old. If you were exposed to 100 a week, multiply that by the number of weeks in a year; and multiply that number, 5,200, by your age, minus 6 years. That's a rough estimate of your exposure to the medium.

In that time frame, you also have viewed advertising in newspapers and magazines, out-of-the-home hoardings, billboards, tweets, banners, direct mail flyers, and brochures. You view web advertising every time you turn on your computer. You are no stranger to the discipline. You may/may not have made a living at it. At any rate, CA will be 'new' learning for you.

You already have a learning curve under construction from the blogs, book reports, term papers, tweets, thank you notes, annual reports, theses, and dissertations you've written in the past.

---

[2] Madison Avenue was/is the address of many New York City advertising agencies.

But a new ideation system? **Plus** a new delivery system?

Conventional wisdom says that having to learn both will slow down and drag out the creative process.

Unconventional wisdom says that you already have skills in place that can be diverted to expand your creativity and shrink the time it takes to come up with ideas. Even more unconventionally, it predicts that you are going to be more creative by concentrating on **process**, rather than **end result**. Read that again: concentrating on **process** rather than **end result**.

If you are a professional in the business, this ideation system will make your life easier. Or so the hundreds of advertising professionals who have been exposed to it at international workshops around the country and the world have said.

You are going to learn CA through four verbal exercises that are interconnected. This interconnection is an innovative addition to, and time-shortening improvement over, the single dimension and random idea starters you most likely have tried previously. Since creativity requires looking at things from a different perspective, they will give you the ability to see things as you haven't seen them before, thereby making new connections. And making them many times over.

For example, in completing Creative Aerobic 1 (CA1), let's say you come up with ten pieces of information connected to the product you're advertising.

You make a list of these ten connections. And in Creative Aerobic 2 (CA2), you come up with ten pieces of information for each of the pieces you found in Exercise 1 (10 x 10). Now, you have 100 pieces of information. All connected to your product, if you'll notice.

Continuing this process, you come up with ten pieces of information in Creative Aerobic 3 (CA3) for each of the 100 pieces found in Exercise 2. Doing the math, that's 1,000 pieces of information. We never take the exercises to that extreme, but it gives you some idea of the wealth of information you can generate.

Creative Aerobics

You will be doing the Creative Aerobic exercises in order. The reason for this? CA1 fuels CA2, CA2 fuels CA3, and CA1 fuels CA4. You are probably familiar with sequential learning. There's no reason to complicate the process by learning the exercises out of order.

A second reason for learning the exercises in order is that you'll be alternating between both sides of your brain. CA Exercises 1 and 3 are left-brain exercises. CA Exercises 2 and 4 are right-brain exercises. By alternating, you can develop flexibility between the two spheres, making it easier and quicker to tap in to your creativity.

OK, let's summarize: you're going to tuck away your current ideation tools. Learn four verbal exercises you may or may not have used before to create advertising, which you have/haven't written before. And do it on demand.

Now that you've digested the premise, and the theory behind it, it's time to get started.

But first: your last two exercises. Number 1 is for your left brain. And your right brain is excited to see what Number 2 has planned for it.

Exercise 11: *Five, Four, Three, Two, One*

In this exercise, you're asked to find twenty five-letter words, that, by subtracting one letter at a time till you reach one letter, you make four different words appear—hence, the title. Although you can deduct a letter from any position in your five-letter word, you cannot rearrange the letters. And you'll need to be careful in selecting words that contain 'a', 'i', or 'o', since you'll be ending with a one-letter word (Are you questioning the 'o'? Think Christmas carols like 'O Little Town of Bethlehem').

Let's start with the five-letter word 'stone'. Remove one letter at a time: stone gives you **tone**; tone gives you **one**; one yields to **on**;

subtracting the 'n' leaves the one-letter word **o**. Let's try another example: stint, tint, tin, in, i. Now you're on your own.

1. 11.
2. 12.
3. 13.
4. 14.
5. 15.
6. 16.
7. 17.
8. 18.
9. 19.
10. 20.

Exercise 12

If you're struggling to find five-letter words that work, try this: start with one letter, your vowel. And then add letters to form words, for example, i, it, sit, spit, split. Notice you can add letters at any point in the word, not just at the beginning. Here's another: a, am, ram, cram, cramp. Try building ten five-letter words, using this technique.

1. 6.
2. 7.
3. 8.
4. 9.
5. 10.

Question: which technique—starting with a five-letter word, or starting with one vowel—felt easier? Did your brain feel differently with each? Which technique was less stressful? Why do you think that is? Here's a more thorough way to explore 'One, Two, Three, Four, Five'.

Exercise 13

Up your game a bit. Run each of your vowels through the twenty-six letters of the alphabet (a, b, c, d, e, d, etc.), pairing them with consonants to form two-letter words. Starting with the letter 'a'. You'll skip 'b' because 'ba' is an abbreviation; 'c'—'ca' is a state abbreviation; and 'd'—'da' is Russian for 'yes'. So your first two-letter word will be 'fa', the fourth note in a music scale. Note the vowel doesn't have to be the first letter. Following 'fa' is 'ga', which is not a word. Your next word will be 'ha'. The next vowel/consonant combination that works will be 'la' (fourth note of the scale), followed by 'Ma' and 'Pa'. Now, restart your alphabet, and make 'a' the first of the two letters. The results: ah, am, an, as, at.

Now, add a third letter to each of the words you found. We'll track our first two-letter word 'fa' through the process. Return to running your alphabet: 'fa-a'? No. 'Fa-b?' Not unless you're referencing a 1950s detergent or a slang word as in 'the fab four' (reference to The Beatles rock group). 'Fa-c', no. 'Fa-d' is a word. 'Fa' plus a consonant also gives you 'fan, far, fat'.

Take these three-letter choices and add a sixth letter. With fad, you can add an 'e' for fade. With fan, you can add a 'g' for fang; add an 's' for fans; and a 'w' for fawn. With far, you can add an 'e' for fare; or an 'i' for fair; or an 'm' for farm. With fat, you can add a 'c' for fact; or an 'e' for feat or fate; or an 's' for fast.

Can you add a letter to your four-letter words—fang, fans, fawn, fare, fair, farm, fact, feat, fate, and fast to produce five-letter words?

Fare gives you fares, fared and flare; fair gives you fairs and flair; fang = fangs; fawn = fawns; farm = farms; fact = facet and facts; feat = feats; fate = fates and fated; fast = feast.

Exercise 14

There are two other stand-alone-as-a-word vowels to address. See how many two-three-four-five-letter words you can find with 'i' and 'o'.

'i'	two-letter words
	three-letter words
	four-letter words
	five-letter words
'o'	two-letter words
	three-letter words
	four-letter words
	five-letter words

In this Brainstretch, each step of how to do it is spelled out for you in detail, as opposed to directions in Brainwork, where you can make choices with how you want to proceed. How did the freedom of Brainwork feel vis-à-vis the structure of Brainstretch? While you maximized results in Brainstretch, was it more confining? Which did you enjoy more?

In the next exercise, let your imagination roam free. There are no wrong answers. In fact, this is an exercise you might want to do more than once.

As you arrive at your answers, see if you feel elated—a little rush of happiness and excitement at finding the unexpected. That's your endorphins making themselves known.

Don't you love the feeling?

Exercise 15: Fill in the Blanks

1. What color is Thursday? _____
2. What does disappointment taste like? _____
3. What is the smell of happiness? _____
4. What do you feel when you touch a cloud? _____
5. What is the sound a smile makes? _____
6. What color would you paint a sneeze? _____
7. If you could taste a dream, what flavor would it be? _____
8. What scent does your birthday give off? _____
9. What sound describes a sunset? _____
10. If you touched success, how would it feel? _____

# Training for Your Creativity Marathon

The purpose of learning CA is to discover how to come up with fresh, unconventional ideas that will cut through the clutter of Internet information overload. So often when advertising a product, it's easy to misinterpret information as the **idea**. And while information can fuel an idea, it is no substitute for one.

You'll begin the learning process by expressing your idea in the form of an advertising headline. It's your creative conduit. But before you can write a headline, you need to have a product to write it about. (And for all those grammar teachers who are clenching their teeth at viewing **another** sentence ending with a preposition: copywriting should read like a conversation on paper. Write it like you'd say it.)

If you were sitting in a classroom or in a creative department, we'd ask you and your contemporaries to empty your briefcases, backpacks, purses, and pockets, and to select an ordinary object to work with: it will be the product that develops your creative insight. Since you're not, we'll make the product selection: a ballpoint pen. What brand? Let's not put the shopping cart before the horse. First, you must learn how to write about ballpoint pens before you can write about a Scripto, Waterman, Paper Mate, Bic, and so on.

Duh. Everybody knows that. Well, not everybody knows that copywriting—the process of constructing the words in an ad—is a craft. Just like making fine furniture. It's how you select your wood—in this case, your words. How you shape them. Assemble them. Polish them. The finished product has proportion. Point of view. Beauty. Text(ure). Impact. And it's memorable. One of a kind.

Take headlines, for instance. Well, not just headlines. When you make a living as an advertising writer—we're called copywriters—it's expected that you will come up with creative writing solutions for a variety of mass media, including print ad headlines and body copy (the text in ads); slogans or positioning lines; radio, television, and video scripts; hoardings/billboards, websites, and social messages; brochures, point-of-sale messages—it's a long list of potential assignments.

We're getting ahead of ourselves though. Let us introduce you to the ballpoint pen. As you've never thought about it before.

For Starters: Where to Begin

Where to begin? Why, on the Internet, of course. You need to find out as much information as you can about ballpoints. So google 'ballpoint pens'.

When were they invented? Who invented them? Why were they invented? Where and when was the patent filed? What's the difference between oil-based ballpoints and rollerball pens? What ballpoint pen is in The Museum of Modern Art in New York City? How much does a ballpoint pen cost? How much does it weigh? Besides writing, to what other uses have ballpoint pens been put? What artists have used ballpoint pens in creating their artwork? How many components are there to a ballpoint pen? How many different materials will you find in a manufactured ballpoint pen, and what are they? What does a ballpoint pen cost? Which was the first country to manufacture ballpoint pens? What was the first store in the United States to sell ballpoint pens? How much did they cost? What year was it that they were introduced?

You can find the answers to those nineteen questions in an online Wikipedia entry.

Exercise 16

What other questions do you want to ask about ballpoint pens? Try asking out-of-the-ordinary questions: Who was the first president of the United States to use one? What do athletes and celebrities use to sign autographs? If you were to measure the amount of writing liquid in a ballpoint pen by drawing a line until it ran out of ink, how long would that line be?

Add your own questions to this list and look up the answers.

Congratulations! You're already on the track of Creative Aerobics 1.

1. First president...
2. Athletes' autograph...
3. Amount of ink...

Your questions:

4.
5.
6.
7.
8.
9.
10.

Space for more:

Creative Aerobic 1 (CA1)—The Facts. Just the Facts

If you researched answers to the questions in the previous chapter, you have a start on a list of facts about the ballpoint pen.

Besides your secondary research, you can also make a list of primary discovery observations about a specific ballpoint. So grab one, study it, and write down what you find—your facts list. How long is the pen in inches? What color is it? Does it have any lettering on it? Is it a rollerball pen or oil-based pen? Don't limit your observations to sight. How does it feel in your hand? Is there any scent to the ink? (Write something and sniff the ink before it dries) When you're writing with it, does the pen make a sound, or is it silent?

The third list of facts about the pen contains your experiences with it. When did you receive your first pen? How did it make you feel? Grown up? Did you ever use it to write on something you shouldn't? Your bedroom wall? Your algebra book? Did you pass notes in class that were written in ballpoint? Did you chew the end of it when you were taking notes or an exam? What did you use it for outside of school?

The fourth list is a list of expressions you know that contain the word 'pen' or words or events associated with it: The pen is mightier than the sword; put your John Hancock on it; signing of the Declaration of Independence; a celebrity signature; can graffiti be done with a pen?

And the fifth list is observations from your friends and relatives. Ask them what they use ballpoint pens for: Do your mom, dad, husband or wife make their grocery list with a ballpoint pen? Does your boss keep a notebook of the miles he/she travels for work, written in ballpoint pen? Does your daughter or sister keep a ballpoint-written personal diary? How important is a ballpoint pen in their lives? What do they like/dislike about ballpoint pens?

Can you think of any more facts or observations?

Sidebar 3

Creative Aerobic 1: 'Facts' About the Ballpoint Pen to Look Up

The ballpoint pen was invented in (DATE).
(NAME) invented the ballpoint pen.
It was invented in Argentina.
It was invented as a portable replacement for the ink pen.
The patent was filed in (LOCATION) in (DATE).
The difference between oil-based and rollerball pens is:
A (BRAND) pen is in Museum of Modern Art, New York City.
The cost of a ballpoint pen ranges from (US$) to (US$).
Other uses besides writing that have been ascribed to the ballpoint pen are:
Artists who have used pens in their art include Andy Warhol, (NAMES).
There are (NUMBER) components to a ballpoint pen.
The materials used to make a pen are (LIST).
The first store in the United States to sell ballpoint pens was Gimbel's in New York City.
The first US company to manufacture ballpoint pens was the Parker Pen Co. (the Jotter).
Ballpoint pens cost US$9.75 in 1945 when they were introduced to New Yorkers.
The first president of the United States to sign a bill with one was (NAME).

Home run hitter (NAME OF ATHLETE) uses a ballpoint pen to autograph baseballs.

Creative Aerobic 1: List of Observations About My Ballpoint Pen

My ballpoint is five inches long with the tip extended.
It is red.
It is round.
The ink is black.
The sides of the pen are smooth to the touch.
It has a name written on its side.
There is a silver pocket clip.
The most unusual use of a ballpoint pen is _____
The ink in a ballpoint pen smells like _____
A list of all the things you can write with a ballpoint pen includes checks, grocery lists, diaries, scorecards, IOUs, etc.
Add your own questions to this list and look up the answers. We'll wait.

Exercise 17

1.
2.
3.
4.
5.

Do you feel you know enough about ballpoint pens now to begin to write headlines about them? Before you begin writing headlines, make sure you have three lists of facts about them: a list of facts you found in secondary research—looking facts up on the Internet; a list of facts you found from observations of a pen you held in your hand and inspected in detail—make sure you used your five senses; and a list you need to make—a list of your experiences with a pen. When did you receive your first pen, and who gave it to you? How did it make you feel? Etc.

Here's space to add any facts that haven't already come to mind: And here's the drill:

> Creative Aerobic 1 asks for a list of facts about your product.
>
> A Creative Aerobic 1 headline asks for one of the facts about your product and adds a twist, either verbally or visually.

The first part of Creative Aerobic 1—the introduction of a fact about the product—is fairly straightforward. Turning to the list of facts about ballpoint pens, let's research an artist who used them in producing fine art.

In the 1950s, expressionist Andy Warhol did a series of shoe illustrations in ballpoint; also, his 'Reclining Male Torso' uses the medium.

Doing a little more research, we can determine the price of a pen in the 1950s—that's when the Parker Pen Company introduced the Jotter long-writing pen for US$2.95. So we now have a fact about the ballpoint pen:

Fact: **Andy Warhol used a US$2.95 ballpoint pen to create drawings.**

We can continue leveraging other facts to create the foundation for more headlines.

Fact: **On the average, ballpoint pens have a two-year shelf life.**

Fact: **Ballpoint pens were first manufactured in Argentina in 1943.**

Fact: **On October 29, 1945, the first ballpoint pens went on sale at Gimbel's department store in New York City for US$9.75.**

You learned more facts about ballpoint pens when you filled in Sidebar 3—facts most likely unknown to the average consumer. Interest, generated by their unfamiliarity, may draw in readers on that basis alone.

The goal of a headline is to be interruptive; to attract the reader's attention; and to draw him/her into the body copy to find out more about the advertised product/service/assignment. The goal of the headline twist is to reward the consumer (for reading the headline) with a desired/desirable context.

But what is the point that the fact is trying to make? What information about the ballpoint pen is it charged with delivering? And also the twist?

Let's examine the fact about Andy Warhol drawing with a ballpoint pen. It's not a fact generally known about the artist. Nor is the fact that quality ballpoint pens cost US$2.95 then. Warhol may have been a starving artist once, who could only afford pennies for his art supplies. But the price of some of his art today is selling for more than US$100 million. It's priceless!

Packaging that in a headline, we have:

Headline: (fact) **Suppose Andy Warhol had used our US$2.95 ballpoint pen to create this drawing.** (Twist) **Priceless!**

Let's explore another fact listed above: In the case of the first department store to sell ballpoint pens in the United States, it may be helpful to know about the ongoing rivalry between department stores Gimbel's and Macy's, one of the fifty greatest business rivalries in 20th-century history. Each strived to be the largest retailer in New York/Manhattan, and the competition was fierce. In fact, a quote of the time asked, "Would Macy's tell Gimbel's?" In this case, it was Gimbel's who wasn't telling, and who wasn't even mentioned in the headline, creating a little mystery for the reader.

Headline: (fact) **On October 29, 1945,** (twist) **there was one thing you couldn't buy at Macy's. For love or for $9.75.**

Suppose, instead of drawing attention to the Macy's/Gimbel's rivalry and underscoring the introduction of the product in just one of the stores, you focus your twist on the date the ballpoint was introduced: October 29, 1945. How would you proceed? And what would you use for the twist?

A thought: October 29 is a date that's gone down in history on at least two occasions: it marked the beginning of the Great Depression in 1929; and the beginning of the transition to pens that supplied their own writing fluid in 1945.

Headline: (fact) **Does October 29** (twist) **ring a bell?**

Here, the context depends on knowing that the crash of the stock market occurred on that day in 1929. And that October 29 is also the day the ballpoint pen was introduced, albeit 16 years later. The use of the colloquial expression 'Ring a Bell' is a reference to jogging one's memory, as well as a reference to the final bell on Wall Street. You may not want to address a negative in your ad. However, often, it can be turned to a positive.

Headline: (fact) **The shelf life of our ballpoint pen is 16 times that of a Hostess Twinkie.** (Twist) **Sweet!**

Once we have the facts, it's relatively easy to turn them into headlines. Ready to try?

Exercise 18

Select five facts about ballpoint pens that haven't been used yet, and turn them into Creative Aerobic 1 headlines:

Fact:
Headline:
Fact:
Headline:
Fact:
Headline:
Fact:
Headline:
Fact:
Headline:

Here's an opportunity for you to see some advertising that our students created once they'd learned their first Creative Aerobic exercise. On the next four pages are ads with CA1 headlines.

MACBOOK AD

The different colors of hands represent the fact that MacBook was introducing different-colored hardware—computer cases in pink, white, etc. The twist: showing different shades of users' hands, rather than the different colored cases.

Creative Aerobics

DUBLIN, IRELAND AD

The Glasnevin Cemetery is 'home' to 1.5 million Dubliners—that's the fact. The twist: not being able to meet them because they are all deceased.

CRAFTSMAN TOOLS AD

The fact is that poor workmanship is often blamed on the tools used to perform the task. The twist is the ad's illustration, a World War II poster of 'Rosie the Riveter', representing competent women who replaced the men who were off fighting the war.

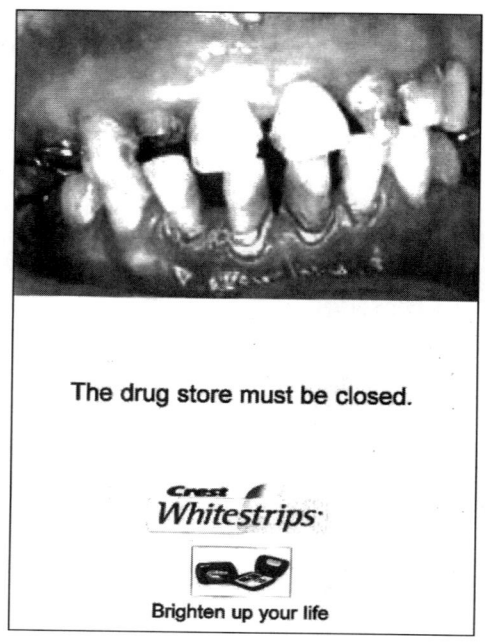

CREST WHITESTRIPS AD

People with bad teeth make what they think are valid excuses for them—"I eat too many sweets;" "I can't find/afford a dentist;" "everybody in my family has bad teeth," etc.—what they think of as fact. The twist: an invalid excuse/fact—drugstores/pharmas are usually open for many hours of the day.

Will this ad be noticed by people with good teeth? The psychology of self-improvement indicates, it will—we're grossed out by the exaggerated, poor condition of the teeth in the photo; it makes us even more eager to take care of/improve the appearance of our own teeth—the purpose of the Whitestrips product.

8 Creative Aerobic 2 (CA2)-New Nomenclature- It Is What It Isn't

In Creative Aerobic 1, you worked your left brain, stretching facts and insight into headlines. Now, it's time to give your right brain a workout.

> Creative Aerobic 2 asks for new what it isn't names for existing objects.
>
> Creative Aerobic 2 headlines regard each new name as a potential headline.

"Aha," you're thinking. "New names? Synonyms." Think again. Synonyms are the what-it-is. You are looking for **'what-it-isn't'** (WII) names, as New England award-winning copywriter Lee Nash calls them. "Antonyms, then?" Opposites may attract. But they also distract. For now, let's try this: select a fact from the Pen Observation List sidebar in Chapter 6.

While you can select any of your lists to work with, observations teach you the process clearly and efficiently. We're going to be listing 'names'. By definition, names mean nouns and we're searching for **concrete** nouns: things that we can see and identify. (Since the concept of a WII is abstract, choosing an abstract name like 'love', 'happiness', etc. doubles the chance of confusion and opens the new name to subjective interpretation. That only confuses the issue, since everyone needs to envision the WII as the same thing, visually, in their minds' eye).

To review our facts: our ballpoint pen is five inches long with the tip extended; it is red, with a silver 1.5-inch bottom section of its case; it is round; it has a clip that attaches to a pocket; a silver clicker button to retract the tip; the name of a company on its side; and the ink is black. There are other observations we can make, but let's work with the ones listed.

The first directive in Creative Aerobic 2 is as follows: now is the time to forget about it—the pen, that is. Concentrate strictly on one of the observations. And make a list of concrete nouns that share the same characteristic.

For instance, we observed that the pen is red. So let's make a list of things that have the color red in common:

an apple	a stop sign	red hair
cherries	Santa's suit	rose
lips	lipstick	a cardinal (bird)
fire engine	nail polish	Legos
heart	hotline	red fox
red squirrel	red velvet cupcake	Superman's cape
Rudolph's nose	red peppers	Red Lobster
clown's nose	Red Sox (Am. baseball)	Redskins (Am. football)
Red Skelton[1]	rare steak	Red Sails in the Sunset
Red, white, and blue	blood	tomatoes
red brick	red wine	red leaves/fall
The Red Door (Elizabeth Arden cosmetics/perfume)	red ants	The Red Book (advertising agencies)
in the red	red balloon	Red Stripe Lager
'Reds' (film)	tomato soup	Red Hat Society
Red Cross	Little Red Schoolhouse	

These have become 'new names' for the pen.

---

[1] American comedian.

Creative Aerobics

Exercise 19

Can you add another dozen red noun/names? Reminder: make sure they are concrete nouns.

1.   4.   7.   10.
2.   5.   8.   11.
3.   6.   9.   12.

Let's try another characteristic: things that have tips.

Tip of the iceberg	wing-tipped shoes	bookie's gambling tip
tiptoe	tip the waiter	fingertip
tip of an arrow		

Let's review what we've done. And what we haven't done.

First of all, there were no restrictions on what we chose, save for the characteristic—all new names shared the same color, pen parts, etc. We could choose any categories for names—animal, vegetable, baked goods, celebrity, fiction, or anything. We could choose an existing phrase that contains the word 'red'—'my bank account is **in the red**'. We could exploit the flexibility of meaning of a word like 'tip' with multiple meanings. By allowing our imagination to run freely, we travel over new territory, not limited by our existing problem-solving skills. And we can enjoy the endorphin release brought about by each new discovery: all our WII 'names' have a connection to our product because they are derivatives of its characteristics!

Are there other ways to come up with new names? Absolutely. We can target how a pen is used. When we write a grocery list, it's a 'dietitian' or 'shopping cart' (You 'cart' the pen along with you to the grocery store to cross off items as you put them in the shopping cart). When we're at a baseball game and keep a record of it in the program, it's a 'scorekeeper'. When we write a letter on paper, it's a 'correspondent'.

We can assign other uses to our pen besides writing. When I (Linda) worked at Young & Rubicam Advertising in New York, I attended a class that the creative department held for new copywriters. We were handed an ashtray (smoking was part of the lifestyle then) and asked to find other uses (names) for it: paperweight, birdbath, paper clip holder, ice cream dish, hammer, etc.

Applying this technique to our pen, if we use the side of it to draw a straight line, a new name for it can be 'ruler'. If we use it to direct a choir, it can be a 'baton'. If we smooth it over piecrust dough, it's a 'rolling pin'. If we use it to do our taxes, it's a 'certified public accountant' (CPA).

With the arrival of fresh, new, WII names, your headline search is over.

Headline: **Shopping Cart.**

Headline: **Choir Director.**

Exercise 20

See if you can come up with ten more new names for the pen, using the same or a different characteristic, and make your case for each:

1.
2.
3.
4.
5.
6.
7.
8.
9.
10.

We have other tools in our CA2 toolbox. Let's try **directed selection**: independent of the pen, create a list of nouns/names that begin with the letter S: scissors, sheep, scotch tape, squash, silk, smoothie, sofa, silly putty, for example.

Here, the names all began with the same first letter. But we can change the criterion: perhaps, make a list of three-syllable nouns: elephant, clarinet, accountant, lasagna, India.

Exercise 21

Now it's your turn. Find your own criterion and list twenty nouns/names that conform to it.

Criterion Tool:

1.	6.	11.	16.
2.	7.	12.	17.
3.	8.	13.	18.
4.	9.	14.	19.
5.	10.	15.	20.

Another tool you can use is **random selection**, where you utilize a series of unplanned results. If you opened the third edition of the *Oxford American Desk Dictionary and Language Guide* randomly, and it opened to page 238, for example, the first concrete noun you'd come across is 'dough'.

Or choose a newspaper/magazine/web article or other information source and select the first/third/seventh concrete noun in the second/last/longest paragraph. Text friends and ask them to send you the first concrete noun they see in the space they're in—you design the randomness.

Exercise 22

Now, describe the tool you plan to use for random selection, and develop a list of random nouns/names.

Random Selection Tool

1.	6.	11.	16.
2.	7.	12.	17.
3.	8.	13.	18.
4.	9.	14.	19.
5.	10.	15.	20.

Ready to discover what new names our students arrived at for their clients? The following ads spell it out for you.

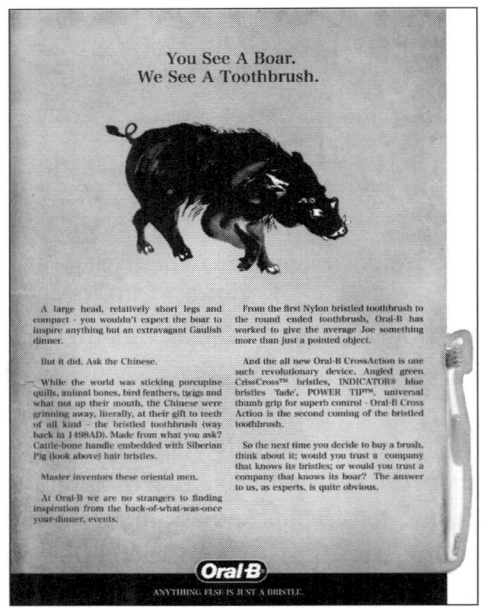

ORAL-B AD

The new name for the toothbrush is a WII: 'boar'—the bristles that are used to make the brush.

Creative Aerobics

PETCO PET TRAINING AD

The new name for pet training is a WII: 'Couples Counseling' refers to husbands and wives with marital issues obtaining advice from a psychologist.

CUISINART AD

The new name for a set of kitchen knives is a WII: 'Toolbox', normally a container for building/construction implements such as hammers, screwdrivers, and so on.

BORA BORA AD

The new name for Bora Bora's shellfish that contain pearls—Jewelry of the Sea.

Creative Aerobic 3 (CA3)–It's the Same. Only Different

Your left brain is awake. And it's very uncomfortable. What's with the WII names? It doesn't make any sense logically. Or does it? Creativity is all about looking for new connections. And our next Creative Aerobic is all about finding them.

> Creative Aerobic 3 asks for the similarities between dissimilar things, that is, similarities between your product (think CA1) and your new name for it (think CA2).
>
> A Creative Aerobic 3 headline follows this template, initially, "Like a (new name), (product) (verb) (similarity)."

Before we plunge into this exercise, let's acknowledge what may not be obvious yet: we can **always** make connections between two dissimilars.

Try this: we are looking for the similarities between a giraffe and a paper lunch bag. We can observe a similarity in color—khaki/brown; they both have 'mouths' (the opening of the bag); they both 'graze' (the giraffe grazes on tree leaves, the lunch bag contains food on which its owner can snack or graze); they both can be found outdoors and in zoos (kids may bring their lunch to a zoo visit); they both have long 'necks' (the sides of the bag, or the upper portion of the soda bottle in the lunch bag); they both can cover a certain distance (the giraffe roams its native grasslands or its zoo enclosure, the lunch bag travels to school); the giraffe has a tongue; the lunch bag has a tongue sandwich; and they both have 'spots' (physical spots on the giraffe; the spots or places where lunch bags are stored, deposited, or sold).

Notice the difference in the type of connections we've made between our first similarity—'color'—and our last—'spot'. 'Color' is a left-brained physical fact. These are the similarities that we are most likely to discover first.

'Spot', however, is more of a right-brained observation of the lunch bag, using a colloquial definition of the word 'spot'. Now we've introduced ambiguity into the equation, and it's about time. Ambiguity is a key element of creativity. The more you practice Creative Aerobic 3 (CA3), the longer your list of similarities will be, the wider their range, and the more you'll enjoy the endorphins that are released by the unexpected similarities you find!

Enough of creative theory. Let's return to creative practice and to constructing CA3 headlines for our pen.

Our first action is to select one of the WII names we came up with in CA2. Let's try 'shopping cart'.

We should be able to construct a Creative Aerobic 3 headline by filling in the blanks of the formula provided in its definition above.

Not so fast!

We have the new name and the product, but that's only two-thirds of the equation. What are the similarities between them? We'll return to our trusty pen and conduct a search.

Similarities between a **ballpoint pen** and a **shopping cart.**

- They both can be made of metal
- They both roll (ball bearing in pen tip; wheels on the cart)
- You can refill them
- You can get a lot of mileage out of both of them
- You can push them (someone who writes all day might be a 'pen pusher'—variation on 'pencil pusher')

Creative Aerobics

- You can find them in Staples or OfficeMax or other retail stores
- They can support you (physically with the cart; financially with a job as a writer)
- They come in different sizes
- Use either one for a period of time and your hand(s) get(s) tired
- You can put the pen in your purse and your purse in the shopping cart
- Pens go on sale; carts hold sale items
- You can find both around the world
- They both can write your personal history (the receipt in the shopping cart chronicles your shopping history; the pen can record your personal history)
- They both can run out (with the pen it's ink; with the cart, it's a shopper in a hurry)
- They're both useful when you're shopping (the shopping cart to hold your purchases, the pen to cross items off your shopping list)

Let's plug a similarity or two into our CA3 formula:

Headline: **Like a shopping cart** (new name), **our ballpoint pen** (product) **rolls** (verb) **smoothly over the items on your grocery list** (similarity).

Headline: **Like a shopping cart** (new name), **you can get a lot of mileage** (similarity) **out of our ballpoint pen** (product).

Headline: **Like a shopping cart** (new name), **our ballpoint pen** (product) **welcomes refills** (similarity).

Exercise 23

Here's your opportunity to find similarities on your own: When listing new names for our pen, we stumbled on 'rolling pin'.

See if you can list at least ten similarities between a pen and a rolling pin.

-
-
-
-
-
-
-
-
-
-

Exercise 24

Now, turn your similarities into CA3 headlines, using your template.

Like a rolling pin, _____
Like a rolling pin, _____
Like a rolling pin, _____

In addition to creating headlines, one of the most effective uses of CA3 occurs when constructing the lead-in to the text of an ad, called body copy. Once you've completed the fourth aerobic exercise, we'll pursue how to integrate this technique into writing your text.

For now, the CA3 headline template should serve you well in honing your skills.

KODAK AD

The similarity between babies/small children (implied by the word 'too') and an adult dressed for work, falling into the water, is that they'll both be wet.

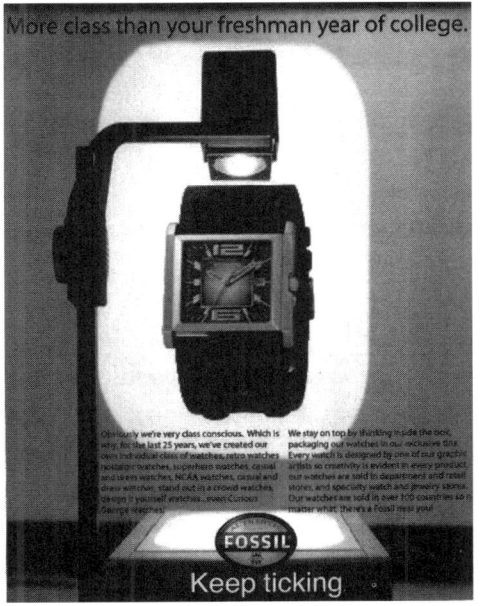

FOSSIL AD

The similarity between a group of students who are taught together and a stylish, chic watch is that they both have class.

Sidebar 4

Are you feeling comfortable using the template in this chapter? With practice, you'll be able to increase your handling of CA3 headlines.

Here are examples of alternate ways they have been constructed.

"The Vikings braved 50-foot seas, gale winds and sea monsters to discover our water. Surely you can manage a trip to the supermarket." (Dissimilar trips to discover the similarity—the water) Client: Akva Spring Water; Agency: Doyle Advertising and Design Group, Boston, Massachusetts (MA), USA.

"You shouldn't have to pass ten gas stations, six burger worlds and a kidney stone on your way to the doctor." (Dissimilar items passed—the geographic landmarks of the trip and the physical ailment of the patient on the way to the similarity—the doctor) Client: Harvard Community Health Plan; Agency: Hill Holliday Connors Cosmopulos, Boston, MA, USA.

"The Mauritius Natural History Handbook lists 174 rare species. Last summer, a visitor spotted Brigitte Bardot." (Dissimilar mentions—Mauritius wildlife and a film star, and the similarity—they're both rare species) Client: Mauritius; Agency: Trikaya Grey, Mumbai, India.

Try them. You'll like them!

# Creative Aerobic 4 (CA4)-Refining Defining

This exercise may provide the most 'Aha!' moments for your creativity. But with three steps to it, involving CA1, the WII aspect of CA2, and its own special element, it's the most complex of the four Creative Aerobic exercises to learn.

> Creative Aerobic 4 asks for new (what-it-isn't) definitions for existing *phrases* (meaning colloquial expressions).
>
> WHAT?????
>
> A Creative Aerobic 4 headline expects the phrase to serve as the headline.
>
> HOW?????

This would be a good time to take a couple of deep breaths. Relax and follow the steps, one by one.

Step 1: Return to our pen. Select the physical and visible aspects of the product, both nouns and verbs that you listed in the CA1 chapter (Chapter 7).

See the sidebar in Chapter 7:

the pen is red, it is round, the ink is black, it has a patent, the sides of the pen are smooth to the touch, it has a name written on its side, the first US company to manufacture ballpoint pens was the Parker Pen Co. (the Jotter), the ballpoint pen is in the Museum of Modern Art in NYC, it has a silver pocket clip, artists who have used pens in their art include Andy Warhol, it has a point, and you use a pen to write/right/rite.

Now what?
Let's reduce our facts list to single words.

RED	ROUND	BLACK	PATENT	SIDE	SMOOTH
PEN	NAME	PARKER	MUSEUM	SILVER	CLIP
WRITE	RITE	RIGHT	BALL	POINT	ART

I capitalized the words so they would stand out and not run together. As we move forward on CA4, they will take on an important role.

Step 2: Make a list of all the easily recognized colloquial phrases that contain these words. Don't make up a phrase—it must be one that everybody knows, and, additionally, knows the true meaning of it.

Now the real work begins. How do you find these elusive words? The Google reference on idioms estimates there are at least 25,000 idiomatic phrases in the English language. In fact, every language has its share of them. The Internet is a great resource for finding them—just google idioms for a selected word. Also helpful is a hard-cover dictionary with 150,000 entries or more—often, it contains idiomatic phrases in the word definitions.

Additionally, check the words following the selected word. Some of them may become phrases for you. For example, the word 'black' in the dictionary is followed by 'black ball (bawl)', 'black bird', 'black board (bored)', 'black head', 'black list', and 'black mail (male)'.

Try not to think about using the well-thumbed softcover dictionary from your school days for this exercise. It won't have enough phrase options in it for you. Honestly!

Ready to get started? Let's begin, once again, with the pen's color—'red'. And this time, when we're looking for phrases, we don't have to worry about concrete nouns, as we did with CA2.

red cent	red eye	red letter day
Red Cross	red carpet treatment	red tape
see red	red herring	red faced
beet red	red-handed	in the red
red ink	red-blooded	red hot
red light	red-light district	

Seventeen well-recognized phrases! That's a great start. Let's try another word—'point'.

case in point	sore point	sticking point
pinpoint	point-blank range	belabor the point
pointless	beside the point	point of fact
miss the point	boiling point	selling point
point of view	on point	breaking point
strong point	brownie points	point out
get to the point	point of no return	point the finger at
point the way	stretch a point	to the point
turning point	on point	a few pointers
point and shoot	West Point	point guard
high point	toast points	low point
tipping point		

'Point' versus 'red': Which word has more meanings? Which word can be both a noun and a verb? The more ambiguity, the more meanings of a word, the more options it's likely to provide.

Step 2½: There's another way to extend ambiguity: that's with homophones—words that sound alike, but are spelled differently, and that have different meanings. Now is a good time to review Exercise 9 in Chapter 4.

When you're up to speed, let's tackle our 'red' phrases. At this point, don't worry about definitions; just worry about finding the homophones.

I've selected four of the thirteen phrases that contain one or more homophones. We don't have to use all or any of them. But once we examine the phrases for this ambiguity, we expand our options for CA4 headlines.

Red cent: Both 'red' (read) and 'cent' (sent, scent) have alternate spellings, producing 'red sent', 'red scent', 'read cent', 'read sent', and 'read scent'.

Red hot: Both 'red' (read) and 'hot' (haute) have alternate spellings, producing 'red haute', 'read haute', and 'read hot'.

Beet red: Both 'beet' (beat) and 'red' (read) have alternate spellings, producing 'beat red', 'beet read', and 'beat read'.

Red eye: Both 'red' (read) and 'eye' (I, aye) have alternate spellings, producing 'red I', 'red aye', 'read eye', 'read I', and 'read aye'.

At this moment, homophones may feel strange to you and not within the realm of possibility. Uh-oh. You've slipped back into your left brain. All speed ahead to Step 3 and your right brain! (Ah! That feels better.).

Step 3: Now comes the time when you take your idiomatic phrase and create a new definition for it that **is directly tied to your product**. And which **is nothing like the real meaning of the phrase**—the same, only different. The secret to success here is looking up or determining the meaning of **every word of significance** in your phrase.

Let's start with the colloquial phrase 'red eye'. In order to create a WII definition for it, you must be absolutely clear about the what-it-is meaning of the phrase. The online Free Dictionary (*Farlex*) defines 'red eye' as 'a long-distance late night air flight'. Obviously, it has nothing to do with our pen. So how do we go about tying 'red eye' to our product?

Creative Aerobics

The connection is going to be the color factor. 'Red' is one of the pen facts we listed in CA1. In CA4, 'red' is one-half of the existing phrase. Now, we're going to stretch its function further, turning it into a synonym for 'pen'. Wherever we SEE 'red', we're going to THINK 'pen'. In other words, to build our new definition, we'll substitute the word 'pen' for the word 'red'.

Our second phrase word is 'eye'. This is the time to look up the meanings of the word—both noun and verb—to find which is relevant in creating the new WII definition.

Eye, the noun, means "organ of sight" (*Merriam-Webster Online Dictionary*).

Eye, the verb, means "to look at or watch closely with interest, to consider" (*Online Dictionary*). For the WII factor, let's work with this meaning.

Generally, in crafting our new definition, we reverse the word order, defining the second phrase word first. So our new definition for 'Red Eye' might be 'looking with interest (second phrase word "eye") at the pen (first phrase word "red," substitute for pen)'.

Hypothetical new scenario/new definition for the phrase 'Red Eye' might be the following: you're in an office supply store, and a red pen catches your eye.

Frankly, we've deliberately overexplained the CA4 process in every monotonously detailed step we could think of. Because what appears simple when you're reading about it becomes a difficult multiphased what-it-is/what-it-isn't exercise that needs to follow Steps 1 to 3 in **exact** order—left-brained thinking, while looking for alternative word meanings; right-brained thinking, while forming WII definitions.

HUH?????

This would be a good time to take a break and refresh the grey matter above your eyebrows. Get a snack. Listen to a favorite song on your iPod, or do a few arm and leg stretches and some shoulder rolls. Relax. R...eeee.........l a x

Practice What We've Preached

Ready to do some more exploring? Let's return to Step 2 above, and select other colloquial phrases to redefine as pen 'WIIs'. We're suggesting five: Get to the Point, Point Guard, Brownie Points, Selling Point, and West Point.

And our choice is…

Get to the Point

We've already completed Steps 1 and 2, identifying the fact (CA1 'the pen has a point') about the pen; and finding a colloquial WII expression (CA4) that references 'point'.

As for the what-it-is meaning of 'Get to the Point' according to the online *Advanced English Dictionary* (AED), it means "to state something directly, as opposed to in a long-winded way."

Now we're ready to look up the individual meanings of the key phrase words 'Get' and 'Point'.

One of the things we look for in CA4 is the ambiguity of meanings—the more definitions a word has, the more are the ways in which it can be reinterpreted. For example, the word 'Get' has one noun and thirty-six different verb meanings listed in the AED. We've selected five that may be operational:

Get: come into the possession of something concrete
Get: cause to move
Get: search a destination
Get: purchase
Get: acquire as a result of some effort

With twenty-six noun meanings and fourteen verb meanings, the word 'point' also contains the flexibility of ambiguity. The most cogent, since it will become the replacement for the word 'pen', is 'the property of a shape that tapers to a sharp tip'.

'Get to the Point' in this context will ask for the order: 'Purchase this pen'.

 Creative Aerobics

Exercise 25

See if you can find new definitions for some of the other colloquial phrases we uncovered that apply to the pen.

Red Eye:

Point-of-view:

West Point:

Brownie Points:

Exercise 26

Are you starting to get the hang of CA4? Let's generate some additional pen fact phrases for you to define.
   Phrases containing the fact **round** are as follows:

Round-up:

Make the rounds:

Round off:

Roundhouse:

Remember that you need to confirm the what-it-is meaning of each of these phrases before you break them down to explore each word's individual meaning. Otherwise, you can slip into writing what-it-is definitions. And that's what you're trying to avoid.

When your fact is a homophone like right/write/rite/wright, keep in mind that the spelling of the homophone will always reflect the product you're creating the new definition for: because you're writing about a pen, it's spelled '*write* of way', not '*right* of way'. However, for the what-it-is meaning, you'll use the original spelling of the phrase—'right of way'.

Exercise 27

Right a wrong
What-it-is meaning: _____
Write a wrong
New what-it-isn't definition: _____

Right or wrong
What-it-is meaning: _____
Write or wrong
New what-it-isn't definition: _____

Civil rights
What-it-is meaning: _____
Civil Writes
New what-it-isn't definition: _____

Right handed
What-it-is meaning: _____
Write handed
New what-it-isn't definition: _____

How do you feel about CA4 now? Did it seem so easy and self-evident when we were explaining it? Do you find that you're now confused? Maybe you skipped a step, trying to take shortcuts. And your new definition turned out to be a what-it-is synonym. Or did you think you knew the definitions of your words without looking them up?

Although CA4 is mostly a right-brain exercise, it does adhere strictly to the left-brain process in creating a new definition for your colloquial phrase.

1. Look up the what-it-is meaning of your phrase.
2. Select the key words in your phrase and look up their what-it-is meanings individually, the more meanings, the better.
3. Substitute your product's name for the CA1 fact word in the phrase.
4. Select the what-it-is meaning of your second word that will best create a new what-it-isn't meaning for the phrase.

Reminder: 'right handed' means putting words on paper with your dominant hand. Its new WII meaning (for write handed) could mean 'You passed (handed) your manuscript—what you had recorded on paper—to your editor'. Or 'you loaned (handed) your pen to someone who needed one'. Not that you 'wrote with your right hand'.

Are you getting it?

A suggestion: Don't create your new definition using any of the words in your actual phrase unless there is no alternative. After all, this is a 'new' definition.

Well, the lesson is over. Time to play. We'll create a chapter of WII definitions for everything we can think of. And then some!

Verbal Four-/For-/Foreplay

The key word in this chapter is 'play'. Throughout this book, we've been playing with words/phrases/language at every opportunity that arose. Now, let's go overboard. We'll fill this chapter with new CA4 WII definitions for existing terms, phrases, and colloquial expressions. The more, the better. And the more easily CA4 will fall into place for you.

We'll start. And then we'll leave spaces for you to fill in. Ready?

Phrase:	New WII Definition:
Taco Belle (Taco Bell)	a girl enjoying food at a Mexican restaurant
Basket bawl (basketball)	crying after your team lost the bb game
Hoarse play (horseplay)	the coach screams until he loses his voice
Cereal killer (serial killer)	finishing off your breakfast of corn flakes
Toe truck (tow truck)	a van delivering shoes to a department store
Back issue	pain that you're experiencing in your dorsal area
Crown molding	tiara covered with a fungus
Tiger woods	an African wild animal preserve
Designated driver	selected golf club
Pedal pusher	bike rider or bike salesperson
Petal pusher (pedal pusher)	Florist (selling flowers)
Water boarding	renting a locker to store your surfboard, etc.
Pressure cooker	fast food chef
Wet (whet) your appetite	get yourself a drink
Venetian blind	an Italian who can't see
Fishing poll (fishing pole)	survey of people who cast baited lines in the water
Fishing Pole	native of Poland catching trout

Cookout (cook out)	chef is missing from the restaurant
Bar exam	checking out a pub or cocktail lounge
Core values	apples on sale at a good price
Lip stick (lipstick)	a brush to outline your mouth
Knit wit (Nitwit)	using needles to create an amusing garment
Hit the deck	slap a pile of playing cards
Pace maker (pacemaker)	drill sergeant setting the speed while leading a hike
Pan handler (panhandler)	dishwasher
Car port	liquor in the glove compartment of your Honda
Hare raising (hair raising)	breeding rabbits
Hair razing (raising)	getting your locks cut off
Boxer rebellion	breed of dog fighting to get off its leash
Japanese beetle	a Volkswagen in Tokyo
Thyme share (time share)	giving your neighbor some of your herb
Thyme's up (time's up)	your herb has sprouted
Pool your resources	throw your valuables into the water
Buy the weigh (by the way)	purchase a scale
Wait (weight) training	learning to stand in line at Walmart
Garden tools	sports equipment used at Madison Square Garden
Pull the plug	remove a wad of chewing tobacco from its package
Shop lifting (shoplifting)	carrying shopping bags filled with purchases
Barber shop	Hair cutter purchasing supplies for his business
Sole music (soul music)	the sound of footsteps
Bear your sole (bare your soul)	carry your shoes
I lashes (eyelashes)	beating yourself up
Braking news (breaking news)	report on recall of cars for equipment problems
Break the record	smash a CD
Executive sweets (executive suites)	Godiva chocolates
Hit the fan	punch a spectator at a sporting event

Verbal Four-/For-/Foreplay

Berth (birth) of the blues — shelf where you store your denim jeans (the blues)
Bring home the bakin' (bacon) — pick up a cake at the bakery
Mini (Minnie) pearl — (a US entertainer) small jewel in an oyster shell
Water under the bridge — soaking liquid for dentures
German shepherd — Bavarian sheepherder

Your turn:

_____ _____
_____ _____
_____ _____
_____ _____
_____ _____
_____ _____

Exercise 28

Fill in the WII definitions:

Clam up _____
Wry (rye) toast _____
Navel (naval) officer _____
Weight (wait) staff _____
Whey (way) bill _____
The back burner _____
Pick of the litter _____
Training weals (wheels) _____

Did you have any trouble finding new meanings for the eight phrases above? Did you check the verb meanings as well as the noun meanings? Did you look up more than one word in each of the phrases? There are some homophones listed—they have the original phrase word listed in parentheses. Use that word when you're looking up the what-it-is meaning of the phrase—don't skip that step.

 Creative Aerobics

Exercise 29

You're on your own. Find phrases and create new WII definitions for them in the spaces below.

It's always a good idea to see how others have handled CA4 in their headlines—our students, for instance. Below are examples of their work.

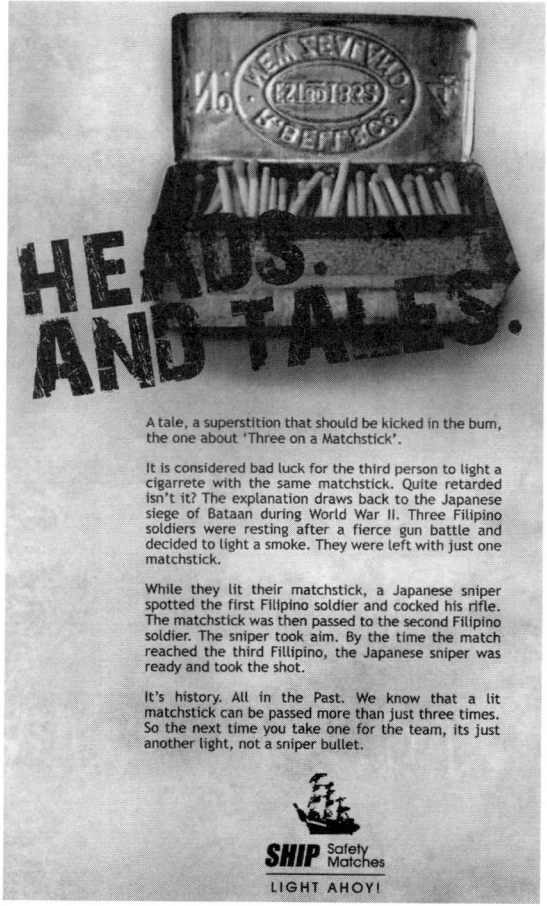

SHIP SAFETY MATCHES AD

The old definition of 'Heads or Tails' is a coin toss, with the side of the coin landing face up being 'heads' and the opposite side being 'tails'.

The new definition of Heads and Tales (homophone for 'tails') is 'stories (tales) about lit matches' (head of the match).

Creative Aerobics

MADRID AD

The old definition of 'The Paint Store' is a retail establishment that sells a colored, protective coating.

The new definition of The Paint Store is 'a repository (museum) for art (oil paintings)'.

THE CZECH REPUBLIC AD

The old definition of 'Checkpoint' (homophone for 'Czech Pointe') is a barrier where security checks are conducted.

The new definition of Czech Pointe is 'a ballerina on her toes in the Czech Republic ballet'.

Creative Aerobics

Body English (It's Not Just About Golf)

The purpose of an ad's headline is to capture readers' attention and invite them to read the body copy.

The purpose of an ad's body copy is to persuade them to buy/buy into your product/service/POV.

One question that immediately comes to mind: How long should body copy be? The answer: as long as it needs to be to persuade the reader.

In Mumbai, India, there are several creatives who try to write a 1,000-word advertisement every year. The challenge, of course, is to make the copy so interesting that people will want to read it. At the other end of the spectrum are ads without any body copy—just a headline. Now it's possible that the illustration or photograph, the graphic design, and the typography are so spectacular that the ad doesn't need any words, and there are occasions when that may be the case. But if you are putting the client's needs ahead of any graphics creative ego, your ad will most likely require body copy.

Today's tendency is to write minimal copy for an ad, but there is a recognized structure for it that contains six steps; and it's to your advantage to learn this.

> Number 1: **your headline.** In my (Linda's) experience, teaching in three different Schools of Journalism (University of North Texas; Northeastern University, Boston, MA; and Southern Illinois University, Carbondale, IL), journalism students, like their professional counterparts, turned in their stories without headlines, which were added by the editor. In advertising, since the headline is the attention grabber, it's essential that you start with it.
>
> In an ad, it's usually the statement that appears in larger type, and it's generally separate from the block of words, called copy.

Number 2: **your lead-in.** This is the opening sentence of your body copy. It either restates the headline or explains it, since CA headlines count on readers' involvement (see Chapter 11). If you're not clear on what you're talking about, people won't read any further.

Number 3: **your transition 1.** Think of it as a 'bridge' between your lead-in and the section that follows. Therefore, it needs to connect—both from an idea and language POV—the lead-in with the main section of your body copy.

Number 4: **your story/sell.** I've double titled this section, which should occupy anywhere from 60 percent to 90 percent or more of your copy. This is where you state facts and features about your products, followed by **their consumer benefits.** Take our pen example. If it fits your hand, what is the benefit? (It's easy/comfortable to write with) How about the fact that you could write a mile and a half of text before your pen runs out of ink. What would that benefit be? It's not enough to merely list facts and features—they usually talk only to your client. The benefits of the product talk to potential buyers, your readers.

I've addressed the 'sell' part of your body copy. The story is the way you weave your facts and benefits together. It may be chronological, like a brief history. It may be in steps, like a recipe. Or it may be functional, like the way your product works. Or...you may have another way of organizing your material. But you want to have a beginning and an end to this section—just like a story does.

Number 5: **your transition 2.** Your body copy has completed its purpose—selling your client's product. But we're not finished yet. We need a second 'bridge' that will connect the story/sell to the final element of the copy, your wrap-up: again, both from an idea and language viewpoint.

Number 6: **your wrap-up.** After the headline, this is the most difficult element to write. Your wrap-up must (a) summarize your copy, (b) pay off your headline, and (c) bring your copy to conclusion.

Ready to tackle this enormous undertaking? Nobody is, the first time. We'll take it slowly. And with a little practice, you will be able to put all the pieces together.

Creative Aerobics

What to Do? How to Do It?

Let's turn back to Chapters 6, 7, 8, and 9, and review the headlines we've written for our product, the pen. Is there one that strikes your fancy? Select it and put it aside for the moment. We've chosen a headline from Chapter 7, a CA2 headline: 'Tip of the Iceberg'. We'll use it to demonstrate the copywriting process.

Wait a minute.

One thing we haven't talked about yet is how we 'see' our ad. Is there a photograph or illustration that comes to mind for this headline? Although you are not the art director who is going to lay out the ad, it's important that you think along these lines. Usually, it is the impact of the visual that hits the reader first. That's only logical, since usually it's the largest element on the page.

Here's some 'copywriter-think' on the subject (with apologies to our graphic design and art director friends): For 'Tip of the Iceberg', we're thinking about how to show the product in the ad. We know we **don't** want to place it literally on the tip of an iceberg—for one thing, the size differential doesn't work—huge mountain of ice; tiny pen.

For another, we never try to illustrate the headline literally—it will fall flat. There needs to be a tension set up between the headline and the visual. One way to do that is to use the substance of the glacier, that is, the snow/ice for the background. The camera would be in close, so there would be some definition of the granular texture. The pen could be placed with its point aimed directly at the camera and photographed from below, to appear larger and more powerful, sort of a bull's-eye effect. This creates visual tension, since we don't really 'see' the iceberg, and the pen is at an angle pointing toward the camera. The close-up (CU) of the textured snow/ice contrasts with the thrust of the pen, particularly when the stuck pen dislodges some of the icy background. This creates tension, too. Here also, the pen in the foreground becomes proportionately larger than its background—the reversal of actual size. This creates tension. And a fourth tension builder is the color saturation of the red pen, in contrast to the greyish-white monochromatic color in the background.

Another way to illustrate the ad might be to 'draw' the pen (with what looks like a pen line) in the snow (Thank you, Photoshop. Now is a good time to color the pen, too.). And then 'write' the headline with the pen. On the snow? Maybe. We'd have to see how it looks.

Or perhaps we 'carve' an iceberg in the shape of the pen.

And ... these are only three thoughts on how to visualize the ad. Your art director will have other ideas.

Back to the matter at hand: your body copy.

Before you do anything else, take the headline you chose apart, and subject it to a thorough exploration, using CA4. Look for phrases that contain 'tip' and 'ice'. And look for phrases that include related words, such as 'cold' (iceberg) and 'point' (tip). Set your goal on finding twenty-five existing phrases that contain an element of the headline. DO NOT EVEN THINK OF GOING ANY FURTHER UNTIL YOU HAVE COMPLETED THIS.

Why? Because CA4 phrases make wonderful lead-ins and wrap-ups.

First things first: let's start looking for them with the word **tip**.

> On the tip of your tongue
> From tip to toe
> Tip your hand
> Tip the scales
> Tip the balance

Then, let's check out the phrases containing the word **ice**.

> Ice maker
> Ice show
> Ice age

Icebreaker
Ice pick
Ice pack
Icebox
On thin ice

Next, let's look for phrases with the word **cold**.

Out in the cold
Blow hot and cold
Cold feet (feat)
The cold light of day
Cold comfort
Cold blooded
Leave you cold

And finally, let's repeat the process for **point**.

Point and shoot
Sticking point
Point and click
Missed the point
Point of discussion
Have we made our point?
On point
Here's the point
All evidence points to
Point you in the right direction
Case in point
What's the point?
Get the point
Point of view
Point of sale
Point of fact

Initially, our headline words didn't generate many phrases. But when we incorporated words related to them, we hit pay dirt—from 'cold' and 'point', from 'tip' and 'ice', we have thirty-six phrases to work with—more than enough. Why extract 'ice' from 'iceberg' instead of using the whole word? If you remember in Chapter 9, we talked about ambiguity. 'Iceberg' doesn't have the flexibility of meanings or ambiguity that 'ice' does. By the way, Chapter 9 also has other 'point' phrases if you want more options.

Once you have your CA4 list of phrases, most of the creative heavy lifting and heavy listing is over. Use them for your lead-ins and wrap-ups. Sometimes they'll help with transitions. But be careful not to overuse them: our creative ego likes to whisper, "Let's try one more. Oh, and here's another great place for one." Pretty soon, we've swapped 'sell' for 'clever'.

Now let's examine our words and phrases to determine which ones could be lead-ins to selling our pen to readers of 'Tip of the Iceberg'.

The Lead-in

Starting with just the word 'tip', we'll need to do a little language shaping to tailor it to work with our headline. So it might read, **Here's a tip on what you need to know before choosing a pen.**

Or **What you need to look for in a ballpoint pen is on the tip of *our* tongue.**

Or **Maybe it's time we covered our pen from tip to top.**

Or **Ready for some cold logic?**

Or **There's a lot of cold comfort in making a smart choice of pen.**

Or **In selecting the best pen for the money, you're not getting cold feet, are you?** (Or…we might save 'cold feet' for the wrap-up: **This is one time you don't have to worry about getting cold feet.**) **If you're shopping for pens, may we point you in the right direction?**

 Creative Aerobics

Or **Case in point: (brand of pen we're talking about).**
Or **It's about time we broke the ice about . . . (some reason tied in to the pen).**
Or **Let's get to the point.**
We could go on and on and on.... And you should be able to too. But we only need one lead-in. So let's move on to our wrap-up.

The Wrap-up

We have a lot of work to do here: (a) summarize the ad content even before the copy is written; (b) pay off the headline; (c) bring the ad to conclusion; and (d) did I forget to mention that you'll need to try to use a CA4 to do this? A wrap-up without the appropriate CA4 may come to an end. But it won't feel like a conclusion.

Well, back to our list of phrases to see what's available.

One solution may be **We're happy to point you in the right (write?) direction.**

Or if we use 'cold' in the lead-in, maybe we use opposites—'warm' or 'hot' in the wrap-up: **No wonder we've got a warm spot in our heart for you.**

Other options are as follows:

Or **In the cold light of day, you'll see you made the right/write choice.**

Or **We're not about to leave you out in the cold.**

Or **Now you get the point.**

Or **All the evidence points to** (product name).

Or **And that may be all you need to know to tip the balance** (Or **To tip the scales in your favor).**

Now that we've compiled a list of possible lead-ins and wrap-ups, we're going to forget about them. We won't be using them until after we craft the story/sell. You'll find that you'll write much better copy by writing it in segments and putting it together later (*Don't* ignore this and try to write copy chronologically).

So far, we've been talking about pens in general, and that's helpful in understanding the CA process. In reality, though, we should be writing about a specific brand of pen, because that is what an agency assignment would be—to write an ad for a specific client. So from this point forward, we'll be thinking and writing about: THE PARKER 'SONNET' BALLPOINT PEN.

The choice of Parker Pens as our client is because it is a well-established, well-regarded manufacturer of quality writing materials. Its founder George S. Parker was born in 1863, and he received his first pen patent 25 years later. You'll want to go online and see what you can find out about the company and about the chosen pen.[1]

You may want to try more sites when you're on your own. Don't google less than three, or you could end up with a body entry like this for the Sonnet pen that we came across:

> The solid gold nib gives high precision and exceptional comfort for every occasion, coupled with a stylish and classic design. Available in a range of finishes, the Sonnet is a work of beauty, emblematic of Parker craftsmanship.

Um…?

Have you heard the term 'puffery'? It refers to empty words—words without substance that form a flattering, subjective commendation and that say nothing much that's specific about the product. What does 'exceptional comfort' feel like? What does 'classic design' look like? And 'a work of beauty'? Give me a break!

This may come as a shock, but writing your story/sell has nothing to do with how you write your headline, lead-in, and

---

[1] Here are the sites we googled:
www.parkerpen.com/en-US/sonnet
http://en,wikipedia.org/wiki/parker_sonnet.html
http://parkerpens.net/sonnet.html
http://parkerpens.net/luckycurve.html

Creative Aerobics

wrap-up. The story/sell is factual, honest, down-to-earth, and benefit oriented.

Pretend you're a journalist for a few minutes. It is your assignment to write an objective account of the Parker Sonnet pen, while pointing out its features. Therefore, you must play it straight. As soon as puffery enters the picture, your credibility and persuasiveness go out the window.

Obviously then, you're going to need facts, facts, and more facts. We found the following facts on the sites listed previously: the Sonnet pen was designed by (fact 1) Geoff Hollington, (fact 2) a London silversmith who worked diligently to fashion an (fact 3) ergonomically shaped pen that incorporated (fact 4) three key design elements—proportion, balance, and elegance. He also concentrated on (fact 5) shaping the pen's cap so that it looked equally good from the front or the back. His attention to detail was such that even an element no larger than one-tenth of a millimeter caught his attention (fact 6). Each pen is hand assembled (fact 7). The solid gold nib comes in a variety of writing widths: extra fine, fine, medium, broad, extra broad, oblique, and italic, so they can be customized to the writer's hand or task (fact 8), and (fact 9) the Sonnet comes in Chinese red.

This is a solid list of facts. How shall we organize them?

Well, we could begin with the history of the pen, followed by its manufacture, followed by its use. Or we could begin on the outside of the pen and keep working our way inside. Or we could let the transition shape our story. There are any number of ways to organize the story: Step by step; Beginning to end; Recipe ingredients style; Guided tour; Chronology; and Sum of its parts. What can you think of?

Now swap your journalist's cap for your copywriter's. It's time to turn facts into benefits. And this is the key: benefits create the story for the reader.

We're going to start by fashioning a lead-in to follow the headline (Tip of the Iceberg). Remember that it must either restate the headline or explain it. We come up with the following: **There's a lot more to the Parker Sonnet Pen than meets the eye.**

In fact, this lead-in closely restates the headline: 'Tip of the Iceberg' means 'There's more to it than meets the eye'. Also, this lead-in gives us the first opportunity to introduce the product by name—its FULL name. The first time the product's name is mentioned in your body copy, you should express it in its entirety. And be sure to mention your product name in the copy. Don't leave it to the visual or the logo to identify it.

Following the lead-in, we're usually required to write a transition that takes us to our story/sell. In this case, the lead-in actually does double duty: it works also as the transition. And that's fine—we'll get to the story/sell a little sooner.

Let's begin thinking about our story/sell by examining the pen: its shape, for example. You may have missed that it's ergonomic, one example of there being 'more to it than meets the eye'. So this may be a way to start: **Take its shape. It's ergonomically designed to fit comfortably in your hand. Almost as if it were made for you.**

The story continues with another observation that is "more… than meets the eye": **And the cap? It's shaped to look equally good from the front. And from the back.**

Now the story goes to the 'submerged iceberg' portion of it— what we can't see: **We hand-assemble each solid gold-tipped Sonnet. Paying attention to details no larger than one-tenth of a millimeter.**

Here's the lead-in/transition and the story/sell so far:

> **There's a lot more to the Parker Sonnet Pen than meets the eye. Take its shape. It's ergonomically designed to fit comfortably in your hand. Almost as if it were made for you. And the cap? It's shaped to look equally good from the front. And from the back.**
>
> **We hand assemble each long-lasting, corrosion-resistant, solid gold-nib Sonnet. Paying attention to details no larger than one-tenth of a millimeter. And providing the width**

Creative Aerobics

of point that works best for you—extra fine, fine, medium, broad, extra broad, oblique, italic.
Which practically assures you we haven't overlooked a thing (Now, you're getting the point!)

As you can see, we went ahead and finished the story. The benefits we attributed to **paying attention to details no larger than one-tenth of a millimeter**—in other words, a tiny amount; followed by **and providing the width of point that works best for you—extra fine, fine, medium, broad, extra broad, oblique, italic**—a matter of personal choice—show the attention to detail that goes into the manufacture of the pen.

The argument can be made that with this amount of attention paid to the pen's construction, nothing has been overlooked. And that forms the content of the transition: **which practically assures you we haven't overlooked a thing.**

And since nothing has been overlooked, the copy concludes with a wrap-up that acknowledges it: **(Now, you're getting the point!).**

In characterizing the roles the wrap-up must play, we listed three points earlier:

1. The wrap-up must summarize the copy. In this case, once the story/sell has clearly spelled out the features and benefits of the pen in detail, the wrap-up, assisted by the summary line of the transition—"Which practically assures you we haven't overlooked a thing"—summarizes its summary by commenting: "Now you're getting the point."
2. The wrap-up must pay off the headline. Since there's more to the pen than meets the eye, which is literally the essence of the headline—there are some features that can't be seen, like the hand assembly; or that are too small to be seen, for example, details like one-tenth of a millimeter in size. Therefore, the copy reaches the opinion by reasoning that "we haven't overlooked a thing", and the reader can conclude

that he/she has gotten the point—the quality of the pen manufacturing process.
3. The wrap-up must bring the copy to conclusion, and "You get the point" is a summary line by content and by definition. Thus, the wrap-up has fulfilled its triple charge.

What's Next?

We're not done yet with body copy. At the beginning of the chapter, we raised the question of how long the copy should be. A good rule of thumb for persuasion-length copy is 100 words or less. If it's too much longer, the reader may cease reading. If it's shorter, it may not persuade. The example we've written is a little longer—105 words.

Suppose we want a faster communication. Can we do it in fewer words?

Let's see if we can edit what we've written: **There's more to the Parker Sonnet Pen than meets the eye. Its ergonomic shape fits comfortably in your hand. Its cap looks good from the front and the back. Each gold-tipped Sonnet is accurate to one-tenth of a millimeter. And with seven point-widths, there's one that fits you. We haven't overlooked a thing (Now you're getting the point!)**

We've cut our copy to sixty-one words. Is it still persuasive?

Let's look at cutting the copy even further: **There's more to our pen than meets the eye: an ergonomic shape. A good-looking cap from any angle. A gold-tipped point in seven widths. All accurate to one-tenth of a millimeter (Now you're getting the point!)**

This edit of the copy is just thirty-nine words. But what about its power of persuasion? Has its brevity reduced its effectiveness? What do you think?

Do you know what the most important, most persuasive word in your copy is? It's the word 'you'.

Note that in the original body copy version, we've used the word 'you' or some form of it five times. In the second, edited version, we've used it only three times. And in the final edit, 'you' only appears once (Does this change your mind about which copy version is the most persuasive?)

Speaking of Style

When you first read the body copy for the Parker Sonnet Pen, did you notice anything unusual about the writing style? Go ahead and reread it, noting that there are incomplete sentences or sentence fragments. That's deliberate: **body copy should read like a conversation on paper.** Write body copy the way you talk. In fact, read your body copy out loud to yourself to see if it rings true: if you wouldn't say it, don't write it. And don't be afraid to take fragment shortcuts to speed up the communication.

The 39-word edit above is predominantly sentence fragments: (a) 'an ergonomic shape', (b) 'a good-looking cap from any angle', (c) 'a gold-tipped point in seven widths', and (d) 'all accurate to one-tenth of a millimeter'.

Notice, however, how parallel construction also is used to smooth this communication: (a) adjective-noun (ergonomic shape), (b) adjective-noun (good-looking cap), and (c) adjective-noun (gold-tipped point).

Another style consideration: It's okay to put yourself into your copy if you do it appropriately. But keep in mind that selling your product comes first.

You may have wondered why we used a set of parentheses above to enclose the wrap-up. Isn't the wrap-up an important part of the copy? The answer, of course, is yes. However, the use of parentheses puts less emphasis, but not less importance, on the wrap-up.

Parentheses soften content. In this case, they say, "We both know that the point we're trying to make is that with such attention to the smallest detail and to even the details you can't see—the 'tip of the iceberg', as it were—you can be confident that we've overlooked nothing in the manufacture of this pen. Get it?" Without the parentheses, the wrap-up would be a little heavy-handed.

This leads us to the next aspect of style to consider: the 'voice' of your copy. What is the tonality you're trying to achieve? In the case of the Sonnet pen copy, the 'voice', or tonality, is quality-oriented conversational. The pen fits comfortably into your hand, "almost as if it were made for you." We "practically assure you we haven't overlooked a thing"; well, maybe we overlooked giving you a choice in the width of pen point, which we now supply. And we toss a conversational tongue-in-cheek wrap-up at you—"Now you're getting the point."

Your tonality, or copy approach, is going to vary, depending on your product and your audience, just as it differs from writing to your grandmother or writing to your boss. If you're writing about a new product, you'll probably strive for an introductory tone that's enthusiastic. If you're writing about a business, bank, or investment product, a more formal approach is warranted: serious tonality, longer sentences, avoidance of contractions, and spelling out of words, instead of using abbreviations.

Getting further into the subject of tonality, technical; medical; scientific; industrial; and agricultural copywriting requires a deeper knowledge of the product at hand—not only in delineating its performance but in the previously mentioned benefit aspects the product offers. If your copy does not read as expert text, it will not be credible, nor more importantly, persuasive to the reader.

Exercise 30

Let's look at opportunities to develop different tonalities in your writing. You fill in the tonalities for each.

Opportunity	Tonality
A note explaining to your daughter's teacher why you forgot to send cupcakes for the party:	_____
A letter to your contractor asking why his bill for laying bathroom tile is 30 percent above estimate:	_____
A letter to the editor of your newspaper concerning bullying in the junior high school:	_____
A note accompanying an overdue bill you forgot to pay:	_____
A card to your brother-in-law regarding the return of a tool he borrowed two years ago:	_____

There is probably a book to be written on the types and uses of tonality in writing, as well as more relevant, literary style tips. We'll leave it to somebody else to follow up.

 How the Student Award Winners Do It

Here's a collection of award-winning ads that University of Florida, Mudra Institute of Communications, Ahmedabad (MICA), and Southern Illinois University, Carbondale students have done, using their CA training.

University of Florida, Runner-up to Best of Show, AAF Student ADDY Awards.

This is a CA4 advertisement for Heinz Tomato Ketchup in its new easy-squeeze bottle. The old definition of 'Natural Selection' is 'An evolutionary process that better adapts creatures to their environment, resulting in better survival rates and more offspring'. The new definition is a 'Spontaneous, better choice'.

University of Florida, Gold Award, AAF Student ADDY Awards.

This is a CA4 advertisement for Zambia National Tourist Board. The old definition of 'Tickle the Ivories' is to 'play the piano'. The new definition is 'Have fun with our elephants'.

Southern Illinois University Carbondale, Gold Award, AAF Student ADDY Awards.

'Ninja' is a new name for hand sanitizer in this CA2 advertisement for Germ-X.

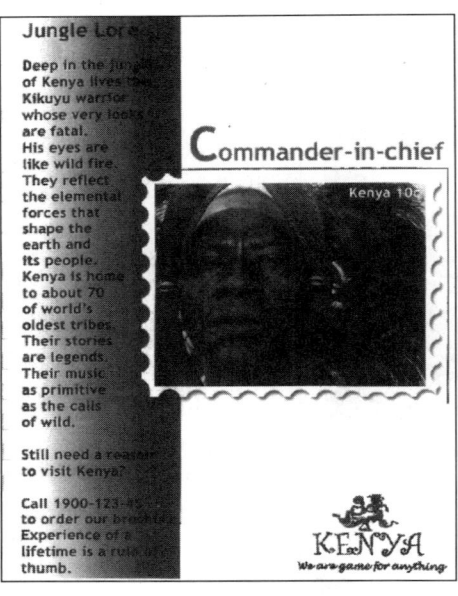

MICA, Silver Award, AAF Student ADDY Awards.

This is a CA4 advertisement for Kenya (tourism). The old definition of 'Commander-in-chief' is 'The president of the United States'. The new definition is the 'Head of an African tribe'.

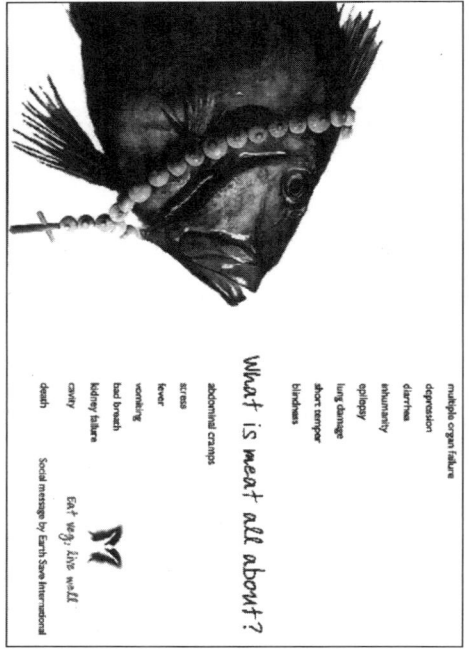

MICA, Gold Award, AAF Student ADDY Awards.

In this CA1 advertisement for EarthSave International, the fact is an explanation of how meat affects our bodies. The twist is that the fact highlights the negative rather than positive effects.

Creative Aerobics

MICA, Silver Award, AAF Student ADDY Awards.

The similarity between a lump of coal and a woman executive in this CA3 advertisement for De Beers (diamond mines) is that they both have maximized their performance when faced with pressure.

 **Creative Laundry List: It's Personal**

Now that you've learned the ins and outs of CA and had an opportunity to view student award-winning work, try your hand at CA, and put a new spin on some of your old and recent favorites:

- Ready for a game of Scrabble? Wait until you see how CA can improve your score!
- Ditto for a game of Boggle. The back-and-forth exercise you completed in Chapter 2 should point the way to considerably more points!
- Don't underestimate your skill with crossword puzzles. Many of them are using easy-to-recognize CA4 clues to fill in the blanks.

- Think of what clever e-mail invitations you can send to friends for your next kitty party (Using CA4 will work purr-fectly!).
- Having a yard sale? Put CA4 to work in your neighborhood signs, and everyone's going to take notice.
- If you're planning a school or family reunion, you'll get high marks for incorporating CA ideas in your plans.
- Family birthdays on your calendar? Your party package will have a lot more presence if CA2 and CA4 wrap up the details.
- Witty tee shirts never get old. Ask CA4 to put words in your mouth and on reunion attendees', family vacationers', and club members' backs.
- Want to increase parent attendance at school conferences? Meet with CA1 and CA4.
- Here's a novel idea: Incorporate your new CA techniques into your personal creativity. See the writing on the wall (and your computer) with your short stories, diaries, plays, articles, song lyrics, other prose, and poetry.

University of Florida, Best of Show, AAF Student ADDY Awards.

The new name for the telltale white 'mask' of untanned facial skin in this CA2 advertisement for Neutrogena Instant Bronze is 'Evidence'.

University of Florida, Gold Award, AAF Student ADDY Awards.

This is a CA4 advertisement for Yellowstone National Park. The old definition of 'Bear with Us' is to 'Have patience with us'. The new definition is 'visit Yellowstone Park'.

Survival of the Fittest.

It's hard to outlive and outlast the competition. Especially when you're ketchup.
New Heinz Easy Squeeze makes ketchup better than the rest.
It's the same quality taste, with no wait, no mess, and no watery stuff.
The new bottle flips ketchup upside-down. Make a superior decision.
Choose Heinz Easy Squeeze.

Making ketchup easy

University of Florida, Runner-up to Best of Show, AAF Student ADDY Awards.

This is a CA4 advertisement for Heinz Tomato Ketchup in its new easy-squeeze bottle. The old definition of 'Survival of the Fittest' is 'To be in the right shape to exist from an earlier time'. The new definition is 'Heinz has been around since 1871'.

Hunt and Peck

Time for a wild goose chase, or at least a wild quail chase? Visit the untapped majesty of Zambia.

Where the African jungle is your backyard.

Your room brings you close to nature. It's made from mud and thatch. You're in for a real treat at dinnertime when professionally prepared "cuisine" awaits you.

Roasted antelope steaks. Fresh chicken. Grilled fish. And the staple of Zambian's diet: *nshima*, a cooked porridge made from freshly ground corn.

It tastes sweet at breakfast. Like mashed potatoes at lunch. Accompanies meat and relish at dinner. It's simply amaizeing!

Beat around the bush with Zambia's nightly entertainment. The social club: locals performing by firelight. Rhythmic singing. Hand-made drumming. Hand plucked piano. And jubilant dancing.

On the prowl for a vacation like no other?

Call 1-800-325-8020

In Zambia, it's always hunting season.

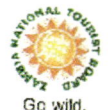

Go wild.

University of Florida, Gold Award, AAF Student ADDY Awards.

This is a CA4 advertisement for Zambia National Tourist Board. The old definition of 'Hunt and Peck' is 'Look for the letters you need on your computer keyboard and type them'. The new definition is 'Track down wild birds and animals in Zambia'.

University of Florida, Best of Show, AAF Student ADDY Awards.

The fact expressed in this CA1 advertisement for Altoids Mints is 'The need for a breath freshener or for refreshment'. The twist is visual—using the proponents in the classic movie *The Wizard of Oz* as they complete their skipping scene on the Yellow Brick Road.

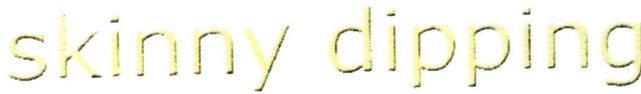

Here's a dessert to sink your teeth into: Nabisco's Reduced Fat Oreo cookies. Dunk them into a tall chilled glass of skim milk. And then drop them into you mouth. And enjoy our crispy rich chocolatey wafers and sweet creamy filling.

And if you are counting your calories, every Oreo adds up to a mere 47 calories and a little over 1 gram of fat per cookie, 50% less fat than the originals.

What a delicious way to have more for less!

twist, lick, dunk and eat

University of Florida, Gold Award, AAF Student ADDY Awards.

This is a CA4 advertisement for Oreo Reduced Fat Cookies. The old definition of 'Skinny Dipping' is 'Swimming nude'. The new definition is 'Dipping your Oreo in a glass of skim milk'.

MICA, Silver Award, AAF Student ADDY Awards.

The fact in this CA1 advertisement for Parker Pens is that an executive who selects a high-quality writing instrument is setting a course for advancement in the corporate world. The twist is visual—it's a photograph of the 'executive', a 10-year-old boy.

MICA, Creativity Certificate, Creativity International Student Awards.

The fact in this CA1 advertisement for MAC (cosmetics) is that the color of its nail polish is more closely aligned to the natural verdant hues of leaves and stems found in the physical world. The twist is that the bottle of polish isn't filled with polish; rather, it's filled with nature's leaves, stems, and buds.

How the Professionals Do It

Until now, all the examples of advertising that you've seen in this book were ads that students created, using the four CA exercises. That's helpful for several reasons: it shows the level of creativity that the process can produce. It also shows the variety of approaches, the individuality of personal styles, and the heightened levels of interest generated—you want to read more.

Let's turn our attention now to some professional work done for actual clients. While we won't be looking at every technique and approach, I've selected ads that follow the CA tenets.

Creative Aerobic 1

Just a reminder: CA1 calls for a fact with a twist.

The first advertisement we'll look at is one for Johnson & Johnson Band-Aid brand.

Let's look at the illustration on the next page. It's a larger-than-life color photograph of one-half of a young woman's face, from her eyebrows to the edge of her chin.

As our eyes move down the page, we notice that she's wearing mascara on her eyelashes, which emphasizes them and draws our focus to her left eye. She's crying, and there's a tear that runs from her eye down along the edge of the Band-Aid on her left cheek, which also appears to be larger than actual size.

Continuing down, we note the texture of the skin on her cheek; we see one-half of her nose, and one-half of her lips.

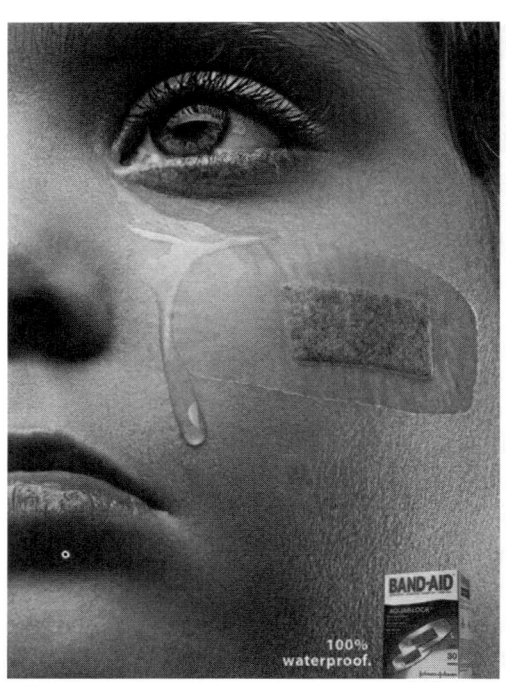

BAND-AID AD
Source: JWT, Sao Paulo, Brazil.

At the bottom of the ad, in the right corner, is a small photo of a Band-Aid box, with the words "100% waterproof."

I'm taking out my creativity magnifying glass and looking more closely at the ad. I notice that the representation of the young woman, her tear, and the Band-Aid application, in larger proportion than they actually are, produces the focal point—the tear running along the Band-Aid. By showing only half the woman's face, which decreases any possibly of identification as well as the level of interest in her as a person, the reader's eye is drawn to the focal point.

The Band-Aid package and the one line of copy have supporting roles in the overall layout.

Now I'm evaluating the ad's elements against our CA1 criteria. The fact is in the only line of copy in the ad: that the Band-Aid is 100 percent waterproof.

What's the twist?

Normally, waterproof items fall into categories such as cameras, cosmetics, hiking clothes, footwear, sports equipment, skiing jackets, gloves, pants, and boots—items that get wet from nature's rain, snow, rivers, and bodies of water. In this case, the twist is that the source of wetness is small and self-contained—it is the eye.

Our second CA1 ad is a public service announcement for the Heineken beer brand.

Its visual treatment is a four-color photograph of a winter woodlands scene (shown here in black and white), with snow covering the ground, and the trees in the background. It is a holiday-timed announcement because it shows a portion of Santa's red sleigh, upended, in the lower left-hand corner; and there are snow-covered, gift-wrapped packages scattered in the snow.

HEINEKEN AD

How the Professionals Do It

The fact, once again the only line of copy in the ad, communicates the message, "Don't drink and drive," because it could result in an accident.

This is a message that is communicated to consumers of alcoholic beverages by manufacturers of these beverages—in general, to drivers of automobiles or motorized vehicles.

The twist in this case is the upended vehicle and scattered gifts, supplying the implication that it is Santa who has been imbibing and has had an accident with his sleigh.

Creative Aerobic 2

Remember, CA2 asks for the creation of a new, WII 'name' for the product.

It shows a photograph of a Mercedes vehicle carrier speeding along a highway, hauling seven new BMW cars, ostensibly to a dealership. The carrier is the dominant element, occupying nearly 50 percent of the two pages. The landscape surrounding the carrier is monochromatic grey in color, which includes the concrete highway at the bottom of the page; and the dark, billowy storm clouds that forecast an impending storm above and behind the carrier at the top of the page.

BMW AD

 Creative Aerobics

The potentially threatening weatherscape sets up visual tension, in contrast to the headline, which reads: "A Mercedes can also bring driving pleasure."

At first glance, you might make the assumption that this is an ad for Mercedes, not for BMW. But the driving pleasure referred to is that of the driver of the carrier, not to the driving pleasure of the soon-to-be owners of the new BMWs on the carrier—a visual WII.

The Nike ad is another visual CA2. Let's start with the headline. It reads, "They keep you alive."

NIKE AD

LEXUS AD

Source: Dentsu Young & Rubicam, Singapore.

Creative Aerobics

'They' is a pair of Nike running shoes. The shoes are photographed on their side in a mirror image, against a white background. Some kind of tubing enters the shot at the top of frame and divides to connect to each shoe, creating an image that looks like a person's lungs (the WII).

So does "They keep you alive" mean the 'lungs' keep a person living? Or is it the exercise one gets in the running shoes that's the life extender?

Creative Aerobic 3

In the Lexus ad, you're looking for similarities between dissimilar things.

The Lexus ad uses four photographs, a predominant illustration of sandy desert flats, and long copy to tell its story.

The headline, "Before we subjected the Lexus to the mercy of the critics, we first exposed it to the mercy of the elements", finds similarities between critics and the elements—mercy.

IF PRINTED WELL, ANYTHING CAN BECOME A THING OF BEAUTY

PRINTED QUALITY

IRL PRINTERS AD

Source: Saatchi & Saatchi, Nyon, Switzerland.

In the IRL ad, a worn and dilapidated scrub brush is photographed beautifully against a textured neutral background. The printing shows exquisite detail in the brush's bristles.

The headline reads: "If printed well, anything can become a thing of beauty." Here, the similarity between the ugly brush and excellent printing production is that they're both things of beauty.

Creative Aerobic 4

This exercise creates new meanings for existing words/phrases.

The headline for this single-page ad, "You need a roll-on with maximum protection," sounds like a line from a 1960s deodorant

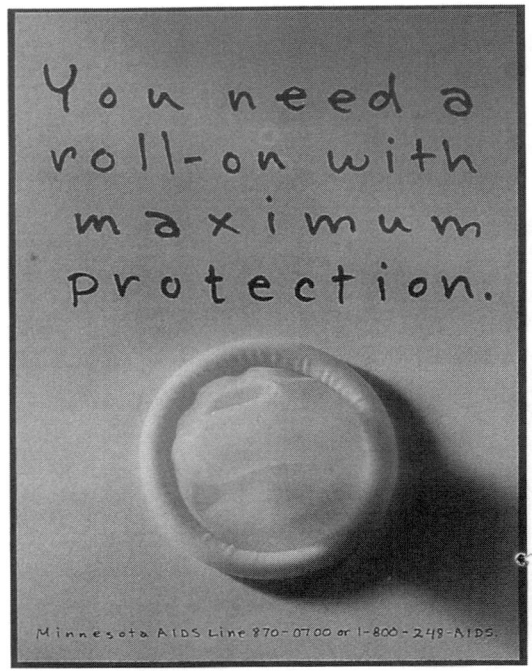

MINNESOTA AIDS LINE
Source: Martin Williams, Minneapolis, Minnesota.

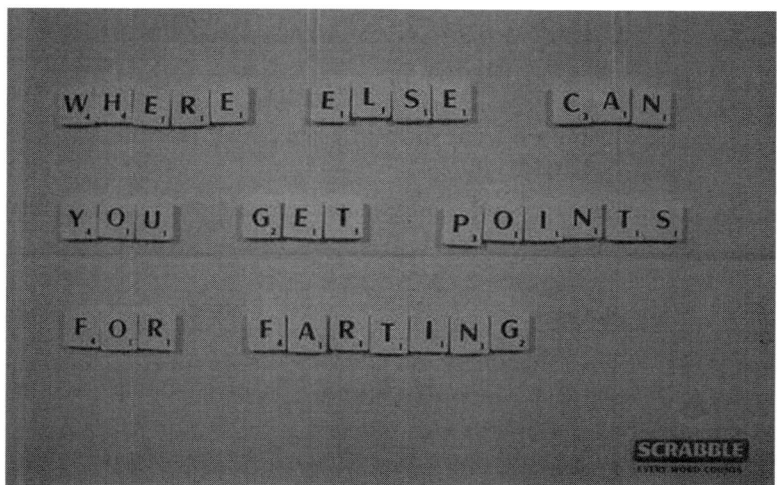

SCRABBLE AD
Source: Ogilvy & Mather, Singapore.

commercial. But it isn't: the headline is hand-lettered above a rolled-up, flesh-colored prophylactic condom on a graduated pink background, advertising protection and a helpline for sexually active people with AIDS.

In the Scrabble ad, while the act may receive an unfavorable reaction from polite society, the term itself is perfectly acceptable, according to the rules of the game and the headline of this ad: "Where else can you get points for farting?"

The word is spelled out using seven of the letter tiles from the actual game, arranged casually against a light-colored background.

 **Creative Laundry List: It's Personal**

In addition to traditional media—newspaper ads, magazine ads, radio and television commercials, hoardings, etc.—there are other applications that will welcome your fresh, creative use of CA.

- If you're a newspaper editor, you'll be turning out eye-catching CA headlines for news stories and special feature sections.
- CA can increase enthusiasm from media editors for your public relations releases.
- Want to contribute more attention-grabbing messages to public service and NGO announcements? Call on your CA skills.
- Post a note to yourself that CA exercises write great headlines for posters!
- CA banners for store openings and bank products can open the doors to more foot traffic.
- Does your company or client require quarterly newsletters? News flash: Put CA4 to work on them.
- CA really clicks when it comes to attracting visitors to company and client websites.
- Should 'auld acquaintance be forgot?' Of course not! And what an opening for a custom New Year's greeting card that companies can send to their clients, customers, vendors, or new business prospects.
- Direct mail gets CA's stamp of approval.
- CA can point you in the direction of point-of-sale materials such as shelf talkers, coupons, aisle caps, etc.

Every Body (Copy) Needs a Slogan, Sometime

Often, in establishing a brand image for their product, companies will opt for slogans. Strategically, we prefer to think of them as positioning lines that create effective and memorable word associations for the product. For example, when you hear 'Just Do It', it brings to mind the sports wardrobe manufacturing giant Nike. 'Das Auto' is the slogan for German automobile manufacturer Volkswagen. The international upscale chain of Taj hotels, resorts, and palaces positions itself as 'the Practice of Perfect Hospitality'. 'It's Better in the Bahamas' is long-established positioning for a Caribbean vacation destination.

Creating slogans is a craft. Since we want people to remember them, we work hard to choose words that fit well together, have an internal rhythm, and/or make people sit up and take notice.

Some things to keep in mind when crafting slogans is to use your English language tools—alliteration, for example. Two of the aforementioned slogans utilize it: the '**P**ractice of **P**erfect Hos**P**itality' (note the internal alliteration in 'Hospitality') in the Taj ad and 'It's **B**etter in the **B**ahamas' for the Caribbean location.

Similes, metaphors, onomatopoeia, parallel construction, opposites, rhyme, ambiguity, individualism, etc. are also effective tools to consider. They can do everything from freshening a phrase, to increasing its memorability, even to mimicking its sound. In fact, the pronunciation of Volkswagen's 'Das Auto' slogan has the harsh, guttural, onomatopoeia of the German language. And don't forget to look for ways to use the CA exercises that you've learned to add your own personal insight to your slogans.

You can also employ psychographics—the way your potential customers feel about your product, its characteristics, or the role it can play in their lives. Have they been avoiding exercise? Physical activity actually improves health. It can lower blood pressure and increase muscle strength. Nike's slogan, 'Just Do It', confronts the inertia and excuses people make for not going to the gym—'I'm too tired'; 'I don't have room in my schedule'; 'exercising is boring'. It challenges them to get over it and 'just do it'—work out! Wearing Nike shoes and clothing, of course.

Volkswagen's 'Das Auto' takes a different approach: one of pride. By translating the article 'the' in its slogan, into the German language 'das', the company strengthens the fact/feeling for customers that they are purchasing a German-made automobile. German manufacturing has a reputation for precision and excellence, allowing purchasers of the car to feel pride in their selection.

Remember that slogans are summarizing generalities that position the brand—the 'umbrella' over it—creating and protecting its identity. Headlines are more specific and may address a single product or product line. Consequently, although not always, headlines in an ad are positioned above the body copy, which delineates and explains them. Slogans, along with the company logo, generally appear under the body copy.

How many words should there be in a slogan? Whatever it takes to communicate the brand's message. However, the rule of thumb is that the less the number of words, the more likely it is that your slogan will be remembered. The Nike and Volkswagen slogans above differ in length: one is two words long, the other five words long, but both are easily recalled.

The length of the slogan, however, isn't the only element that you need to pay attention to; also consider the number of syllables per word. 'Just Do It' has three one-syllable words, optimal for quick communication. 'Das Au-to' has one one-syllable word and one two-syllable word, a total, also, of three syllables.

Keeping these guidelines in mind, let's review the phrases we've come up with in previous chapters. With a little tweaking, we may find that some of them can serve as slogans/positioning lines for our Parker Pen.

Parker Pens: You Get the Point. (Chapter 12, four-word slogan, four one-syllable words)

Parker Pens: Just Point. And It Clicks. (Chapter 12, five-word slogan, five one-syllable words)

Parker Pens: Point of Fact. (Chapter 12, three-word slogan, three one-syllable words)

Parker Pens: A Strong Factor in Civil Writes. (Chapter 9, six-word slogan, four one-syllable words, two two-syllable words)

Parker Pens: A Strong Presence in Civil Rites. (Chapter 9, six-word slogan, four one-syllable words, two two-syllable words)

Parker Pens: For the Write Handed. (Chapter 9; four-word slogan; three one-syllable words, one two-syllable word)

We can also review the facts we learned about the pen. Historically, the Parker Pen Company was founded in 1888. So its pens may have been used to document some important events.

Parker Pens: Writing History for More than 120 Years. (Two-word slogan, one two-syllable word, one three-syllable word)

Parker Pens: Recording History Since 1888. (Four-word slogan, two one-syllable words, two three-syllable words)

Parker Pens: Documenting America for Generations. (Four-word slogan, one one-syllable word, three four-syllable words)

Parker Pens: Signing of the Times. (Four-word slogan, three one-syllable words, one two-syllable word)

Parker Pens: Signature of the Times. (Four-word slogan, three one-syllable words, one three-syllable word)

Parker Pens: Our Sign Language Since 1888. (Five-word slogan, four one-syllable words, one two-syllable word)

From the examples above, it's clear how efficiently and effectively CA can tackle the job of writing slogans.

Exercise 31

Ready to try your hand at coming up with slogans? In Chapter 12, there are nine separate facts about the Parker Sonnet Pen that are listed. See if you can create ten positioning lines based on them:

1. Parker Pens:_____
2. Parker Pens:_____
3. Parker Pens:_____
4. Parker Pens:_____
5. Parker Pens:_____
6. Parker Pens:_____
7. Parker Pens:_____
8. Parker Pens:_____
9. Parker Pens:_____
10. Parker Pens:_____

The Pros' Prose

Here are some slogans from existing advertising campaigns that demonstrate how CA principles could have been used in the creation of them.

Creative Aerobic 1 Slogans: Facts

Ivory Soap

There are a variety of ways to harness a campaign to facts. The simplest way is to simply state the fact. And that's what the forerunners of Procter & Gamble (P&G) did in 1882 with Ivory soap. They announced that it was "Ninety-nine and Forty-four-one hundredths-Percent Pure." Touting the unadulterated composition of the product sold millions of cakes of Ivory soap.

Nickelodeon TV

This commercial cable television channel, primarily directed at children and adolescents, was launched in New York City on December 1, 1977. It also took a simple approach to its slogan, positioning Nickelodeon factually as "The First Kids' Network."

The J.M. Smucker Company Jams and Jellies

It was in 1897 when Jerome Monroe (JM) Smucker introduced the first of his fruit spreads. The name 'Smucker' was unusual, and the company's advertising agency seized upon this fact for its slogan: "With a Name Like Smucker's, it has to be good."

Head & Shoulders Shampoo

American-headquartered Procter & Gamble (P&G) first put its antidandruff shampoo on store shelves in 1961, marketing it under the slogan "You Never Get a Second Chance to Make a First Impression."

Although the word count of its marketing slogan—eleven words—flies in the face of conventional recall, there is an inner rhythm construct here. Read the slogan aloud, emphasizing the capitalized words:

--/ ---- --/ ---- --/ ---- --/ ---- --/ ---- --/ ---- --/ ---- --/
you Ne- ver Get a Sec- ond Chance to make a First im- Pres- sion

By 1982, Head & Shoulders had become the number one shampoo brand. Was its success due to its slogan?

M&M's® Candy

These little morsels of button-shaped, chocolate-filled candy shells jumped on the market in 1941. Named after the last-name initials

Every Body (Copy) Needs a Slogan, Sometime

of the company's founder (Forrest E. Mars—M) and the son of the president of Hershey's (Bruce Murrie—M), who had a 20 percent share in the product, M&M candy had a distinct advantage over its chocolate-covered competition. And it became the company's slogan: "Melts in your Mouth, not in your Hands."

Notice the use of alliteration in the slogan—coincidentally, 'melts' and 'mouth' are 'm' and 'm' words.

Creative Aerobic 2 Slogans: New Names

7UP Soft Drink

This lemon–lime flavored noncaffeinated soft drink was launched two weeks before the Wall Street Crash of 1929, not the most auspicious time to introduce a new product! Its long-running slogan invented a WII name for the brand, 'The Uncola', which translated into noncaffeinated competition for both Coca-Cola and Pepsi soft drinks before either product had a caffeine-free version.

Esso/Exxon Gasoline

Esso first used the image of a tiger in its advertising after the World War II, when the company was looking for a way to differentiate its brand of gasoline from the others on the market and to create a visual presence of power for a product that could not be seen when it was dispensed at the gas pump.

'Tiger' became the new WII 'name' for gasoline; and Esso's slogan, "Put a Tiger in Your Tank," became one of the best-known campaigns in advertising.

Skittles Confectionery

In 1974, the manufacturer of this brand of fruit-flavored sweets began production in the United Kingdom, and it didn't take long for it to cross the 'pond'. America has enjoyed its sugary variety since 1979. If someone invites you to "Taste the Rainbow", most likely it isn't a rainbow you're being offered, it's Skittles.

Creative Aerobic 3 Slogan: Similarities Between Dissimilars

State Farm

The mutual insurance giant was founded in 1922, originally to protect the automobiles of farmers. In the rural culture of the United States and other countries, farmers have always depended on the friendliness and assistance of their neighbors when they needed help. The company's best-known slogan, "Like a Good Neighbor, State Farm is There," finds the similarities between good neighbors and an insurance company—they look out for you, they help you in bad times, they're dependable, they're close at hand, they can visit you, you can visit them, etc.

Creative Aerobic 4 Slogans: New Definitions for Existing Phrases

Morton Salt

In 1911, Morton Salt introduced its first advertising campaign bearing the slogan, "When it rains, it pours" in *Good Housekeeping* magazine. The original meaning of the phrase refers to the belief that when something good or bad happens, it usually occurs repeatedly and within a short time frame.

The alternate meaning of the Morton slogan is that when the weather is humid (salt can absorb moisture, which causes it to stick together), it still pours freely out of the package or saltshaker.

The slogan is in the Advertising Slogan Hall of Fame.

Corona Beer

In the late 1970s, this beer brewer developed a television advertising campaign using animated bubbles to tell a carbonation story for the brand: "Every bubble's passed its fizzical." The company created a made-up homophone—"fizzical"—which substituted for the word 'physical' in the military's qualification for joining the service: 'passed the physical'. In other words, it meant 'a medical examination to determine the individual's state of health before enlisting'. Corona's new meaning of the phrase is that 'the carbonation in Corona Beer is bubbles of gas'.

Taco Bell Fast Food

This American chain of fast food restaurants based in Irvine, California, serves a variety of Tex-Mex food to more than two billion customers annually in its 7,000 restaurants. Its 2014 slogan, "Think outside the Bun", a variation on 'think outside the box'—meaning 'come up with fresh ideas'—has an alternative meaning: 'consider options other than food served on a bun for your meal choice'.

Exercise 32

Here are additional slogans that conform to CA or English language tools criteria. See if you can identify which CA could have been used for each:

Client	Slogan	CA
1. British Rail	We're Getting There	
2. Federal Express	When it Absolutely Positively Has to be There Overnight	
3. Timex	It Takes a Licking and Keeps on Ticking	
4. AT&T	Reach Out and Touch Someone	

Creative Aerobics

5.	Coca-Cola	It's the Real Thing
6.	Wrigley's Gum	Double Your Pleasure, Double Your Fun
7.	Calvin Klein's	Between Love and Madness Lies Obsession
8.	Mountain Dew	Do the Dew
9.	Kay Jewelers	Every Kiss Begins with Kay
10.	Taco Bell	*Grande* Taste. *Loco* Value
11.	Metropolitan Life	Have You Met Life Today?
12.	General Electric	Imagination at Work
13.	Perdue	It Takes a Tough Man to Make a Tender Chicken
14.	Taco Bell	Live *Mas*
15.	Pork	The Other White Meat
16.	Sharp	Sharp Minds, Sharp Products
17.	Peter Paul Mounds & Peter Paul Almond Joy	Sometimes You Feel Like a Nut, Sometimes You Don't
18.	Office Depot	Taking Care of Business

(Answers at the end of next chapter.)

# Mass Media Medley

So far, the only medium we've dealt with in depth is print advertising. And there's a reason for that: many of its principles will apply to other media, some more than others.

Since this is primarily a book on accessing your creativity, we'll describe traditional media you may want to learn more about. And then provide websites where you can access examples of them.

Hoardings, Billboards, Outdoor Boards, Transit Shelters

In a sense, these media resemble a print ad with visual and headline, although without body copy. They're posted outdoors, along roads, bus routes, highways, on shelters, and on buildings. And sometimes they contain just typography and a logo.

Billboards may range from static signs to lighted boards to LED digital billboards that change the advertiser's identity every few seconds.

Since cars, vans, trucks, lorries, and other vehicles are moving when they pass them, the typography is large enough to be read easily and quickly. And the number of words should be limited—less is more (impactful).

Generally, we use outdoor media in two ways: to enhance the brand, with an **image** and headline, or to indicate at an exit the **directions** to businesses, fast food and restaurants, historic sites, local features, parks, and activities.

Here's how we can adapt work we've already done on the Parker pen to create a hoarding, or two:

Let's say you decide to post an image hoarding/billboard on the outskirts of affluent cities that do business in English, for example Mumbai, London, New York, etc. Your idea, or concept, is to have two boards, the second following the first.

For your visual treatment of the first board, you combine calligraphy with a photograph of a hand beginning to letter '*M*', '*U*' on it with an enlarged Parker pen. The letters are huge and exquisite. There may be a penciled guide diagram around them, like scaffolding on a building, indicating the board is under construction.

The visual treatment of the second board reveals the completed name of the city in calligraphy. Underneath '*M U M B A I*' is a headline:

Parker Pens: You Get the Point. There may be room for the logo; there may not. However, you've typeset and included the product name in the headline.

Maybe you're so enthused with this concept, you decide to add a third board. So you leave 'MUMBAI' and the line 'You Get the Point' on the second board, but remove the brand name and save it—Parker Pens—for a third board. Your calligrapher creates the logo to appear under 'Parker Pens'. And a photographer takes a picture of the name and logo to appear on board three. Why bother to photograph general artwork for the third board? The artwork is flat and two-dimensional. Studio lighting will give it more dimension and presence when posted.[1]

Television Commercials

An important way that television differs from other media is that it appeals to more than one of your senses at a time. Consequently, you

---

[1] If you'd like to observe examples of outdoor media, access the following website: https://designshack.net/articles/inspiration/50-creative-and-clever-examples-of-outdoor-advertising (Retrieved December 2, 2016).

need to consider both—what you're going to show on the screen, and what your viewer is going to hear, when you're concepting a commercial.

Here are some practices to avoid:

1. Avoid 'wall-to-wall' audio—words that occupy every second of the commercial. They have a way of distracting and detracting from your visual.
2. Avoid 'talking heads'—static spokespeople who just stand there and talk. That minimizes the medium, and is generally ineffective in capturing audience interest.
3. Avoid visuals that bombard the viewer with multiple scenes of the target audience's lifestyle. They tend to sell lifestyle instead of your product.
4. Avoid shoehorning your product into a commercial. Instead, present the product as hero; otherwise, you're undervaluing both the product and the viewer.

Television is especially effective as a medium for demonstrating your product in action—something you can't do in newspapers and magazines. You can use it effectively for telling a story about your product. And when it comes to message retention, think about the 'mind-sticking' properties an effective television commercial enjoys. Viewers will 'remember' seeing a commercial that hasn't run in months.

Here are some guidelines to keep in mind when you're creating television commercials:

1. Keep it simple. Use your creative magnifying glass to get inside your visual and maximize it. One idea explored in depth is more effective than superficial exploration of a dozen visual ideas.
2. Make your first scene audience-involving. You used to have four seconds to capture your viewers' attention. Not anymore.

3. Be bigger than life. Exaggerate. Get as close to your product and the action as you can. If you stand back at a safe, medium distance, you'll never really come in contact with your product. And neither will your audience.
4. Although it's possible to cram seventy-five words or more into a 30-second TV script, don't. Try to say everything in forty words or less. Let your visual do the talking.
5. One idea per commercial. No exceptions.
6. When you're thinking up ideas, think of ways to produce them. If you do not have a clue as to how you'll pull them off, rethink them.
7. Use CA to add style and richness of detail to your ideas.
8. Use sound effects and music backgrounds to add drama and interest to your ideas.

When you're writing for television, you need to know its terminology in order to create a clear picture of your idea in script form. Utilize the following terms to convey your ideas.

Basic Television Terminology and Definitions

SCRIPT FORMAT: the typed, two-column explanation, and designated execution of a television script, listing what is seen and heard in a commercial.

VIDEO: the title of the left-hand column, a descriptive list of scenes that identify both the action content and the camera angle. The title is underlined. This column is single spaced and typed in all capital letters.

AUDIO: the title of the right-hand column; a list of the sound content of the commercial, including the announcer, script, sound effects, and music, if included. The title is underlined. This column's spoken words are typed in upper and lower case. Directions and production notes, such as the person speaking—usually an announcer—are typed in all capital letters and abbreviated: ANNCR. The announcer may be speaking **on camera**—ANNCR (OC). Or the **voice** may be heard **over** the picture—ANNCR (VO). Directions for music will appear in capital letters—MUSIC: IN THE CLEAR (meaning 'up, full volume'). Sound effects will appear in caps, abbreviated, and the directions spelled out—SFX: BIRDS SINGING.

ESTABLISHING SHOT (ES): the first scene of a commercial. It is described in detail to provide visual context and establish the shooting location(s).

LONG SHOT (LS): camera is at a distance from the scene that is being shot. This shot can be used to create visual context by identifying the location.

MEDIUM LONG SHOT (MLS): this shot splits the distance between the camera and LS. If there is a person in the shot, the camera is back far enough to show him/her in totality, from head to toe, approximately ten or more feet from the camera.

MEDIUM SHOT (MS): this shot captures a person from the knees up. The camera is approximately six to eight feet from the subject.

MEDIUM CLOSE-UP (MCU): this shot captures a person from the waist up. The camera is approximately four to six feet from the subject.

CLOSE UP (CU): this shot captures a person from the shoulders up. The camera is approximately two to four feet from the subject.

EXTREME CLOSE UP (ECU): this shot has a lot of impact. The camera is two feet or less from the subject and may show only a portion of the subject or scene. The first of the professional advertisements that you looked at in Chapter 13—the Band-Aid ad—used the impact of an ECU of the young woman's face to draw attention to the photograph. In fact, the face was bigger than life size.

Sometimes when you're shooting a commercial, you have more than one person in the frame (in view). If you have two people, it's a TWO SHOT. If you have three people, it's a THREE SHOT.

Creative Aerobics

And so forth. Of course, if you have sixteen Bollywood dancers and singers on-screen, I think I'd just go with LS!

If you have two people talking on camera, you may want to show each from their individual POV. Let's say the camera is positioned behind the first person, capturing the second person. When the camera moves to the opposite spot, behind the second person, to pick up person one, it's called a ONE-EIGHTY (180). In other words, the camera would be 180° from its first position. That's an effective way to shoot dialogue.

The camera can move in other ways. It can:

ZOOM IN: here, the camera moves toward the subject, shortening the distance of the shot. If it's a rapid movement, for example, zooming from LS to an ECU in just one or two seconds, it's called a SNAP ZOOM. When the camera moves in the opposite direction, it's a ZOOM OUT, where you widen the shot by moving the camera away from the subject.

If you do it quickly, it can be a SNAP ZOOM.

Sometimes you want the camera to follow a subject or action that's moving in a direction: left, right, up, or down (I suppose the camera could move diagonally, but for simplicity's sake, let's concentrate on these four directions).

PAN LEFT has the camera moving left; PAN RIGHT has the camera moving right, and so forth. One additional direction you might want to consider is a 360° PAN, where either the camera travels completely around the object being shot, or the object turns completely around in front of the camera lens.

Once you've finished recording all your shots, either on film or videotape, it's time to edit your FOOTAGE, the number of feet or meters of film/videotape you've shot. I'm only going to talk briefly about editing it to arrive at your final project—the commercial.

If your footage is action oriented, you're most likely going to want to move from scene to scene by using a CUT—that's where you electronically sever the end of a scene and electronically 'glue' it to the next shot. CUTS are an effective tool for setting the pace of the commercial. If you think your commercial will work better/be more interesting if it's fast-paced, you'll use more/shorter shots. If you want a slower pace, you'll use less/longer shots. And if you're trying to build suspense, you'll start with lengthier shots and alternate them, each time making the sequence shorter and shorter.

1----------2----------1---------2---------1------2------1----2----1---2---

I've noticed lately that most commercials on the air are edited with cuts. Maybe it's because our lifestyle has gotten faster.

There's an alternate tool to use in editing your footage. If your commercial has emotional content, or if you want a gentler 'feel' to it, you'll consider using a DISSOLVE or cross-fade—decreasing the saturation of color and brightness in the present scene as you fade up on the saturation of the scene that follows. How long should you make your dissolve? To answer that, it's time to do a little math.

Usually, we edit on videotape, so if we've shot on film, we'll transfer the footage to tape. A tape has thirty individual frames or images per second. A ten-frame dissolve lasts only one-third of a second. That's very short; more often than not, it will be referred to as a SOFT CUT.

I prefer longer dissolves. A one-second dissolve is thirty frames. A three-second dissolve is ninety frames. Some years ago, a 30-second beer commercial used only one dissolve, but it lasted through the entire commercial, beginning with a couple sitting in the cockpit of a moored sailboat at sunset having a beer and dissolving to a CU of the bottle of beer. I'm estimating that it was a 900-frame dissolve!

Creating a Television Script

Remember the hoarding we created for Parker Pens at the beginning of this chapter? Let's see if we can turn it into a 30-second television commercial.

Creative Aerobics

Script for Parker Pens TV Commercial

VIDEO	AUDIO
ESTABLISHING SHOT: OPEN ON A BLANK SCREEN	MUSIC: CLASSICAL, IN THE CLEAR WHITE SCREEN
MEDIUM SHOT OF HAND REACHING IN FROM THE LEFT SIDE. IT BEGINS DRAWING THE LETTER 'M' USING CALLIGRAPHY	
BEGIN A SLOW ZOOM IN ON THE LETTER.	
ECU OF IT. NOW THE CAMERA PANS RIGHT	
IT FOLLOWS HAND AS IT BEGINS DRAWING	MUSIC: UNDER
CAMERA HOLDS UNTIL 'U' IS COMPLETE.	MAN (VO) PUZZLED: I don't get it ...
PAN RIGHT, FOLLOWING HAND	MUSIC: IN THE CLEAR ... UNDER
CAMERA HOLDS UNTIL 'M' IS COMPLETE.	MAN (VO): I still don't get it ...
PATTERN CONTINUES FOR THE 'B' ... AND FOR THE 'A' ...	MUSIC: IN THE CLEAR
AND FOR THE 'I'	MUSIC: UNDER
CAMERA PULLS BACK TO SHOW WORD HOLD ON 'MUMBAI'	MAN (VO) SURPRISED: OH!!! I get it!
HAND WITH PEN REACHES BACK IN FRAME	ANNCR (VO): You got the point, obviously. And once you get the point, get ... the point!
PUSHES PEN AGAINST BOARD. IT STICKS	
SUPER: PARKER PENS GET THE POINT.	MUSIC: IN THE CLEAR ... OUT.

Would you like to know how long television commercials run in length?

Mass Media Medley

In the 1950s, most were 60 seconds long. In the 1970s, advertisers cut the length to 30 seconds. And today, the standard unit is a 15-second spot. But is it the hardest working unit?

Industry professionals like David Ciccarelli believe that the most effective length for creative, memorable, and engaging TV commercials is 30 seconds. And I agree with him.[2]

Although I mentioned earlier that you can fit seventy-five words in a 30-second commercial—we read at approximately two and one-half words a second—wall-to-wall words suffocate the action and interest in the visual content. Think about using forty words or less. The commercial script above has twenty-two words—nearly half of that.

You'd probably like to watch some commercials in action.[3]

Radio Commercials

Radio has often been called the 'Theater of the Mind'. With auditory—voices, music, and sound effects alone—you can create anything you can imagine: a volcano that erupts, tossing carrots, and clarinets over the countryside. Two hundred and one Dalmatians peeling off their spots and turning them into chocolate chip cookies. The Seven Dwarfs auditioning two new members for their family, named Messy and Psycho. And...

Radio uses auditory effects to create action, drama, emotion, exaggeration, humor, fantasy, nostalgia, science fiction, and so on. No photographs. No illustrations. No special effects. No documentaries. No film. Just the pictures that form in your head from what you hear.

---

[2] Retrieved December 2, 2016, from voices.com/blog/effective_length_for_TV_commercial, 6/25/14

[3] A site for television commercials that aired in 2016 on Super Bowl 50, retrieved December 2, 2016, from youtube.com/watch?v=Q2c2mprcpw

For your radio commercial, let's work again with the Parker Pen material we've already developed, putting the ideas in our head into the ears of listeners.

Since the hoarding/billboard concept of using the Parker Pen to inscribe in calligraphy the names of major cities, and to post them at the cities' outskirts, is a visual concept, and we will use only sound—no pictures—let's develop a scenario of the action for it first:

SCENARIO: An announcer is standing in the middle of Mumbai traffic about to broadcast an event—the first time a calligrapher has ever attempted to design a hoarding by climbing a ladder and drawing it on the board, using only a single writing instrument.

As he begins to speak, a crowd gathers. Individuals in the crowd begin commenting on the action as it is happening.

SFX:	MUMBAI HIGHWAY TRAFFIC—AUTOS, RUMBLING LORRIES, TOOTING HORNS, WHIRRING BICYCLE-POWERED CARTS, BLEATING GOATS, AN OCCASIONAL ELEPHANT TRUMPETING, IN AND UNDER
ANNCR:	(IN A LOW, WHISPERED REPORTER'S VOICE) …. Today, we're on the outskirts of a city … where an artist is going to complete a hoarding … using nothing but a single writing instrument …
SFX:	GATHERING CROWD, GETTING CLOSER AND CLOSER
ANNCR:	A crowd gathers as he begins his climb. Let's watch …
SFX:	(EXAGGERATED) FOOT STEPPING ON WOODEN LADDER RUNG
WOMAN 1:	(SPEAKING LOUDLY) …. Look! (CROWD QUIETS DOWN, UNDER)
	(SHE SOUNDS EXCITED) He's climbing the ladder …
MAN 1:	(EXCITED, TOO) It's 12 meters tall, if it's a foot!
	(SHOUTING TOWARD CALLIGRAPHER OFF MIC) Be careful!

Mass Media Medley

SFX:	CREAKING OF WOODEN LADDER AS CALLIGRAPHER CLIMBS ALL THE WAY TO THE HOARDING
ANNCR:	(HUSHED BUT EXCITED) He's reached the hoarding board. And he has something in his hand!
CHILD:	(EXCITED) It's a pen! He's drawing!
SFX:	LOUD AND FAST SCRIBBLING OF A PEN, MAGNIFIED SOUND IN THE CLEAR … UNDER
MAN:	(PUZZLED) I don't get it.
WOMAN:	It's a very beautiful BIG letter! (CROWD MURMURS THEIR APPROVAL)
SFX:	CIRCULAR SCRATCH OF PEN, IN THE CLEAR … UNDER
CHILD:	It's a capital 'M' … with a curlicue!
SFX:	SCRATCH OF PEN CONTINUES UNDER
WOMAN:	'M' … 'U' … 'M' …
MAN:	(UNDERSTANDING, IN UNISON WITH THE WOMAN)
	'B' … 'A' … 'T' (MAN ALONE) …… Oh, I am getting the point!
ANNCR:	(CROWD SOUNDS OF SURPRISE, UNDER) And I am making a point about the precise, proportioned, balanced, and elegant writing pen by Parker. Parker Pens: Get the point!
SFX:	MURMURING CROWD, APPLAUSE, TRAFFIC RESUMES, DROWNING OUT CROWD.

The most effective radio commercial length is 60 seconds. In order to allow time for sound effects to register, it's best to keep your commercial under 125 words.

Now it's time to lend an ear to some effective radio commercials. Dick Orkin's Radio Ranch[4] has been producing award-winning work for many years. It's an excellent introduction to radio production.

---

[4] Retrieved May 17, 2017 from radio-ranch.com/our-work

Creative Aerobics

Answers to Slogan Questions in Chapter 15

1. CA4
2. CA1
3. Rhyme
4. CA4
5. CA4
6. Repetition
7. CA4
8. Alliteration
9. Alliteration, CA4
10. Span./Tex-Mex
11. Repetition, Mnemonic
12. CA2
13. Opposites
14. Spanish Lang. for Tex-Mex
15. CA1
16. Repetition, Mnemonic (product name)
17. Repetition, Rhyme
18. CA4

# 17 .Com Creativity

Technology is always changing, Creativity never does.

—Linda Conway Correll George on Creative Aerobics verbatim, 2016

While writing about the history of advertising, Keith Reinhard, Chairman Emeritus of DDB worldwide, claimed that in the last 60 years there have been many power holders, agencies, CEOs, brands, and individuals, and they have all risen and ebbed. But the one element that has been at the apex of power in the advertising world is the POWER OF AN IDEA. He goes on to say that in today's age, true creativity is more powerful than ever. And he notes that influences come and go, but ideas always endure.

Unlike the power of an idea, which is timeless, technology is not. It evolves constantly. Traditionally, advertisers have used newspapers, magazines, radio, and television as carriers of their marketing messages. However, with technological advances, devices such as cell phones, tablets, laptops, and PCs have overtaken them. Increase in the use of personal hand-held electronic devices have enabled advertisers to reach individuals, regardless of time and location. And it's reflected in how advertising dollars are being apportioned.

"2016 is the year when digital media ad sales, 'estimated to be almost $70 billion' (Katz, 2016)[1], finally equal television ad sales"

---

[1] Retrieved from http://www.forbes.com/sites/brandonkatz/2016/09/14/digital-ad-spending-will-surpasstv-spending-for-the-first-time-in-u-s-history/#30efaca6959c

(MAGNA US Advertising Revenue Forecasts, October 2016). Beginning in 2017, digital media ad sales will occupy the largest percentage share of total advertising revenue—more than 38 percent. Overtaking television ad sales is a major milestone. Television's strength has been its ability to attract and retain the undivided attention of a population watching the same show at a given time, making it relatively easier to target that market segment. On the other hand, digital media emphasizes and accepts the viewer as an interactive participant, with the ability to choose what to watch, when to watch, and how many times to watch.

However, this advantage comes with its own set of challenges; such as how to stand out from the clutter, how to capture viewers' attention, how to wrestle with them to take the time necessary with the content, how to generate interest, how to guide the prospect from eyeballing to clicking and ultimately to purchasing, and perhaps the most daunting challenge of all is finding ways to deter ad blocking.

In 2016, ad blocking was expected to result in a loss to advertisers of US$41 billion. This has definitely raised concern and caution among advertisers globally. "It had to get big enough to be an important issue, and I think we've reached that inflection point," said David Moore, Chairman of the Board of Directors for Tech Lab within Interactive Advertising Bureau.[2] As reported in an article by Stacey Rudolph (2016),[3] there were 198 million active ad blockers globally (in June 2015).

In such a user-friendly advertising-unfriendly environment, the most effective weapon that advertisers can have is a creative idea. And with CA, there is no time wasted in coming up with results.

---

[2] *Advertising Age* (2015). "IAB Explores Its Options to Fight Ad Blockers, Including Lawsuits" September 4. Retrieved 21 June, 2017 from http://www.adageindia.in/digital/IAB-Explores-Its-Options-to-Fight-Ad-Blockers-Including-Lawsuits/amp_articleshow/48809669.cms?from=mdr

[3] Rudolph, S. (2016). The State of US Digital Display Advertising [Infographic] *Business2community*, September 8, 2016. Retrieved May 19, 2017, from http://www.business2community.com/infographics/state-us-digital-display-advertising-infographic-01649203#qg3omDUxCRBisIG7.97

Follow CA1 and you've generated a list of facts for your assignment. Follow CA2 and you have a list of new names for it. Follow CA3 and you've formed a list of connections between CA1 and CA2. Follow CA4 and it will take you to solutions you never would have thought of without it. Now manipulate those layers of information to arrive at creative solutions. Note that the use of plural—Creative Aerobics enables you to find multiple ideas quickly and easily—is extremely helpful in the 2.0 world.

By harnessing the power of creativity, an advertiser can persuade a prospective customer not only to view the company's marketing message but also to act upon it.

Display or Banner Ads

Display or banner advertisements occupy prime real estate on a website. They are hard to miss and are traditionally static. Due to clutter and their static treatment, their efficiency in communicating the marketing message is diminishing.

CA1, CA2, and CA4 can be used directly to efficiently increase their effectiveness in generating interest and higher click throughs. Additionally, CA4, with its humorous twists on meanings, can increase brand memorability as well as the number of click throughs.

There is documentation to back this up. For example, I (Arpan) was instructing a class earlier this year on how to use CA to prepare an advertisement for the Edwin The Duck brand that would appear as a static display advertisement in its LinkedIn campaign. During the first six days it ran, this student advertisement generated 1.8 million impressions, six times the number generated by a more conventional approach.

Search Pages

Today, sponsored search results are often designed to look like the 'real' thing, making it harder for viewers to distinguish between the

two. However, search engines must mention 'Ad' in the beginning to avoid misinformation and misrepresentation. In general, sponsored advertisements are monotonous and offer very little incentive to engage.

Facts with a twist (CA1) can make a difference here in enabling click throughs. And New Names (CA2) can be used as a valuable resource pool for Google AdWords bidding (creating a list of new names can optimize bidding).

Social Media

With over 1.6 billion active users presently, Facebook is by far the largest online social network. Additionally, it is available in an app format for smartphones and tablets.

Facebook offers both static and dynamic forms of advertising. Display advertising tends to be more static; advertising embedded in the news feed is more dynamic and video based. All four CA exercises can be used here: print ad formats for static applications, and television commercial formats for dynamic applications.

LinkedIn, Twitter, and Instagram offer similar choices for implementing display and text options. Another major player that offers similar choices along with some additional options is YouTube, which allows banners and videos (of different lengths, skippable, and unskippable suggestions).

Lately, Wendy's, the fast food chain restaurant, has been using Twitter and YouTube to promote itself and gain popularity and followers among its target audience. Wendy's started using its Twitter platform to engage in an exchange that is popularly known as 'roasting' with their customers. As a strategy, Wendy's began roasting/responding with a healthy dose of sass in its retorts. This approach became an instant hit among its target audience and started getting attention and recognition. Followers started liking and retweeting these roasts. YouTube videos were created, capturing reactions of individuals who were shown some select responses of Wendy's on

Twitter. Through this campaign, Wendy's gained many more followers and was successful in repositioning itself uniquely in the minds of its target audience as a brand with a healthy and positive personality. CA can be immensely useful in such short-term promotional efforts by brands. CA1, CA2, CA3, and CA4 can be applied skillfully in the crafting of instant immediate and healthily sassy responses.

Websites, social networking sites, apps, and other upcoming mediated information and communication platforms will continue to discover unique and novel ways for advertisers to promote their products and services. Although skills and strategies that are successful today may become obsolete and unsuccessful tomorrow, the one skill that never goes out of fashion or demand is that of creativity. By using CA, an individual can not only sharpen his or her creativity but can also transform into a one man/woman army; coming up with multiple creative ideas in a short amount of time; and continuing to succeed in the constantly evolving and sometimes mutating ecosystem of the .Com.

# Practical Reflections on the Profession

Through seventeen chapters, you have wrestled with your creativity and practiced putting it to work. You've tossed out ideas. Thrown sales pitches and slogans back and forth. Run headlines around in your head. Caught yourself smiling and beginning to think up new definitions for phrases like 'Lieder (Leader) of the Pack'. And contemplated connecting more dots for .com.

Your right brain is accelerating its output—faster, faster! It's outpacing your writing hand. Whoa! Slow down. And, for a moment, let's reexamine why you've put the lesser-used part of your brain through such an extensive and stimulating workout.

We asked Professor Subhash Tendle, Professor, Crafting Creative Communications, MICA, and former Creative Director at FCBUlka, Mumbai, for his take on the importance of creativity. He's worked in the advertising industry for more than three and a half decades, selling products from saris to soaps. Now he sells hope instead of soap, helping people design their careers in visual communications by holding workshops for professionals, consulting, mentoring, sculpting, and illustrating. Here is what he told us:

This is the Age of Creative Thinking. Many thinkers, such as Philip Kotler and Daniel Pink, have said this in different ways. They say, after the Agriculture Age, which was followed by the Industrial Age and the Information Age, we are witnessing the Creative Age. And for good reasons.

Rickards (1985)[1], referring to Alvin Toffler's Future Shock, said that '...an increasing number of problems have no precedents, and there are

---

[1] Rickards, Tudor (1985). *Stimulating Innovations: A Systems Approach*. London: Palgrave Macmillan.

fewer tested ways of approaching them. This poses problems for organizations. Many suggest that creativity is indeed the answer . . .'

My apologies if I use too many quotes in this document, or sound like a research paper advocating Creativity-in-Management Studies, but I firmly believe that "Man is not a circle with a single center; he is an ellipse with two foci. Facts are one, ideas are the other." I wish I'd said that, but it's actually a quote from Victor Hugo's Les Miserables.

It is understood that the left side of the brain does the function of analytical or logical thinking, and the right side controls our emotional/creative thinking. The fact is, we need both kinds of thinking abilities in life. But over a period of time, probably due to our education system, we have grown to depend more and more on analytical/rational/thinking.

Logical thinking normally uses a path where every question has to be answered either 'Yes or No', 'This or That', or '1 or 0'. Traditional logic comprehends only that which is consistent and noncontradictory in nature. Life, however, is defined by ambiguity—inconsistency and contradictions are the hallmarks of human existence. Therefore, using only logical methods can affect our innate thinking patterns, our ability to be creative.

After all, how long can one succeed using only one-half of our brain's resources?

Ideally, one should start learning this as early as possible; unfortunately, our education system does the opposite. That's why Picasso said, "Every child is an artist. The problem is how to remain an artist after growing up." Or to quote Mark Twain, "I was born creative, but my education cured me."

Creative thinking is not necessarily restricted to the arts and crafts as it is generally understood. It is required to be taught in every discipline in schools and colleges. The reason for including creativity, innovation, and creative problem-solving in our curriculum is because they are essential skills today! In fact, many believe they are intrinsic skills!

There is empirical evidence to support this. I quote from the Routledge College textbook on this topic: "Creativity is considered to be a vital asset for anyone who is in a leadership role. . . . Creative leaders actively hunt *for new problems and are especially successful in handling new challenges, which demand solutions outside the routine of orthodox strategies. They often possess significant vision and are able to inspire others by their creative talents."*

A recent research document supports this point of view: 'Creativity and innovation are the buzz words in today's organizations. The pressure of continually developing new processes, products, and services at a faster speed to stay ahead of the competitors has left no choices for organizations but to embrace the path of creativity and workplace innovation' (Ghosh, 2014).[2]

Unfortunately, most management institutions focus mainly on analytical thinking and tend to mold students into 'trend followers'. But the fact is, more often than not, when one can identify a trend, one is already too late. In fact, what we need is a method to help us create a trend, rather than one that will help us merely to identify one. This is where creativity and innovation come in—breaking the mold and making a difference.

One of the foremost researchers on creativity, Paul Torrance, said, "Whenever people confront a problem for which they have not learned and practiced solution, some degree of creativity is required." His summation is as good as (that of) A-Day-in-the-Life-of-a-Manager—"Creative thinking is the process of sensing difficulties, problems, gaps in information, missing elements, something askew; making guesses and hypotheses about the solution of these deficiencies; evaluating and testing these hypotheses; possibly revising and restating them; and finally communicating the result." Isn't this what management is really all about?

I am reminded of what Plato said eons ago, "Life must be lived as play . . ." The ancient Greeks knew that play (or creative activity) was the secret of learning. Their words for play (paida) and education (paideia) are only slight variations of the same theme.

My firm belief, and it's based on a lifetime of experience, is simply that: Play is the way all animals and children learn. It's a powerful catalyst for the development of mental and physical skills. In fact, mastery of almost

---

[2] Ghosh, K. (2014). Global Journal of Flexible Systems Management 15: 169. doi:10.1007/s40171-013-0049-2

any skill comes from approaching it with the openness and enthusiasm of a child—it is the Method of the Child that makes learning possible.

As adults, we are repeatedly admonished that taking a 'playful' (my term for 'creative') approach will be dismissed as 'not serious; frivolous'. It's ironic that what adults often dismiss as 'child's play' is actually a very serious activity—you may have noticed that when children are pursuing their own agendas, their powers of concentration are prodigious!

Ironically, the naysayers seem to believe that a tense and miserable demeanor gives observers and onlookers the impression that hard work is being done. The truth is that seeming to be overserious is a warning sign: watch out for mediocrity and bureaucratic thinking!

In my experience, I've found that people who are truly serious about mastery and high performance are secure and confident enough to lighten up, to let go. But to 'let go', we need to create an environment where it's safe to be serious about the importance of play.

To reiterate, I believe that it's important to create a special environment for students that fosters innovation and creative thinking.

Today's business environment has already implemented it—here, innovation is not only a matter of survival; it's big business! For example, in 2013, the United States Patent and Trademark Office estimated that the value of intellectual property to the country's economy—patents, trademarks, copyrights, creative solutions, etc.—was more than $5 trillion! With stakes in the 'business of ideas and innovations' this high, can we afford to ignore them?

My humble submission is that we need to add creativity and innovation as core topics to the curriculum. They could be further broken down into methods—random association, redefining of the problem, SCAMPER, mind mapping, to name a few.

Linda's (author Correll George) Creative Aerobics is one such time-tested method to enhance the creative powers of the brain. In developing Creative Aerobics, Linda has figured out how to combine play and work in a unique manner. At MICA, we have been practicing that for some time, and its effects can be seen—particularly in the award-winning work of our students!

Maybe you'd like to hear more about it from three of MICA's award winners, who employ CA daily in their work at well-known international advertising agencies.

Prasad Venkatraman

Prasad's advertising background is multinational. He is a veteran of McCann Erickson, where he was featured in the agency's Creative Showcase, and of BBDO. He is no stranger to international competition, receiving awards at Cannes and from AdAsia Pacific. Presently, he is Creative Director of Lowe Lintas and Partners Advertising, Mumbai, where he teaches the CA ideation system to his staff.

Here is what he said:

"Creativity is a science! No, it's an art!"

Perhaps this may be the only other question, after "Why did the chicken cross the road?" that has boggled the mind of many a scientist for centuries. Obviously, the question has many answers, so let's delve into something far simpler: Creative Aerobics.

While it seems like a child that Don Draper and Richard Simmons conceived "One dark and stormy night…" Creative Aerobics just allows the mind to limber up and consciously fuse the left and right sides of brain together. It consciously asks, "If it's one brain, why can't both the sides work as one?"

Whether it's logic, deductive reasoning, lateral thinking, random patterns, or just elementary, dear Watson, Creative Aerobics allows the train of thought to either be on time, or to skip a few rudimentary stations altogether. That's all fine and dandy, but does it make sense? Of course it does. At first, it feels like learning to ride a bicycle; but after years, it feels just like riding a bicycle several years later. It helps you to open new compartments/windows/horizons/perspectives/problems when you have been handed an advertising brief. You automatically are engulfed by a plethora of information that helps you assimilate and break the whole thing down into juicy little titbits you can use. And if you have been doing it as long as me, it's all happening while you assimilate the brief during the briefing process itself.

Now the real question you are wondering (I hope!)—Does it have any practical implication? If you see a long and prosperous career in advertising ahead of you, yes. You should see if Creative Aerobics will work for you; if it allows you to convince someone why an idea makes sense. Let's say you want to defend an idea in front of a client, your art partner, or worse, your boss. If you have followed some of the exercises, you can either make sense to a logical person or seem brilliant to the creative one. It's because you can then make them traverse through the same stations you did while thinking of the headline, the tagline, the film, or even if it's a web banner. (Yes, really! A web banner!)

Some of the finest examples of how Creative Aerobics works would be (to) tell you what my relatives thought . . . (it was) I did for a living.

Relative X: "Oh, so you are a copywriter? Did you study law?"
Me: "What?"
Relative X: "Don't you copyright stuff?"
Relative Y: "Copywriter? Ha ha! Does that mean you copy stuff?"
Me: "Ha ha! Never heard that one before!"
Relative Z: "Copywriter? So do you work with Xerox?"
Me: "Yes, what would you like me to photo-copy-write?"

Don't even get me started on what I had to do when I became a creative director. But you get the drift. People associate a word with objects or activities that revolve around them or their lives. The trick is in finding the word that appeals to them. Then the next word. Then the next. Put them together, and you have your headline, the tagline, or even your web banner. (Yes, really! Really!)

I know right now it sounds like a stretch. But that's exactly what Creative Aerobics is. It allows you to expand your mind and give it that little amount of flexibility that our government could use right now. So set that morning or evening alarm (as you please!), brush off that negativity, and get ready for that set of exercises that allows you to have a rather 'healthy' idea.

Now, ask me why I am trying to be funny and informative at the same time. I don't know. (Maybe it's because) I've been using Creative

Aerobics to fuse my left and right brain together (for so long)—for more than a decade!

Elrid Carvalho

Elrid thinks of himself as just another ordinary bloke with incredibly ordinary thoughts. Case in point: as he wakes up every day, the only thought that bounces around in his head to the whirring soundtrack of an electric toothbrush is, "God, please do not let me suck today."

He has been doing this every morning for over a decade. He's also won a bunch of awards—Cannes Lions, The One Show, Clio, to name the usual suspects, and there are some unusual ones, too.

Elrid is currently a Senior Copywriter at TBWA Advertising in Singapore. Here's how, when, and why he uses CA:

"It's been done before."

Those four words are known to be the most powerful of all idea killers in the advertising industry. Yet we clock in every morning, sometimes just in time for lunch, to keep coming up with new ideas and solutions to a client's marketing problems.

But hearing it day-in, day-out, day-in can have a stifling effect on creativity. This sometimes leads us to ideas we creative kinds think to be genius, only to receive the soul-crushing, "It's been done before" response.

The truth is, we agency creatives do not use creativity because it is more fun for us (which it definitely is). We use it because it increases the effectiveness of our advertising. Creativity works as an amplifier. And that is the be-all.

I have been doing this for slightly over a decade now. Still, most mornings the blank sheet on my Word document feels like it is going to win. That is when the lessons in Creative Aerobics from way back in 2005 kick in. And that blank Word document and I have a stare-off that ends up in victory for me.

These long-ago lessons have paved richer paths to arriving at creative solutions. Yes, plural. Because there's nothing more constraining to the creative process than holding on dearly to one single idea. A constant

Practical Reflections on the Profession

search for better is the crux of being a good creative. But do not stop at good. Push to become a great creative.

From all that I have learned in the last decade as an advertising creative, this stands to be true: Never stop after Round 1. If you do, you are giving up on the chance of coming up with ideas that push boundaries and break conventions. It is only then you will end up with the ideas that stand at the opposite spectrum of... well... you know... 'It's been done before'."

Broti Ganguly

Clueless about what she wanted to do after graduating with an Honors in English Literature from Lady Shri Ram College for Women, Delhi University (DU), but with absolute clarity about what she didn't, Broti Ganguly quite accidentally stumbled upon the world of advertising and landed in Mudra Institute of Communications, Ahmedabad (MICA) in 2004, in the Crafting Creative Communications Programme. After eight enriching years at JWT (J. Walter Thompson) Advertising and another two years at Grey Worldwide, both in Kolkata, Broti is now working as a Brand Design Manager at R K SWAMY BBDO. Broti is the recipient of a Silver ADDY Award from the American Advertising Federation (AAF), Gainesville, Florida, USA.

Broti eloquently captures the pain and pressures advertising professionals face in trying to come up with ideas:

Imagine being trapped (read a brainstorming session in a 'bored' room), and only an idea can save you. You have no access to the 'net.

Or your brain has gone into freeze mode after hours of working on a thankless, mind-numbing task. And there is a juicy brief waiting to be cracked. Wait a second, there is no brief really... only a deadline!

"Why don't I have an idea already?" That voice in your head screams hysterically, which by the way, no one but the ideas on their way can hear. Terrified, they quickly slink away into some dark corner of your brain... waiting for you to cool down.

The truth is our brain needs exercise. We don't think enough anymore. Everyone googles everything, and Google dutifully throws up similar

 Creative Aerobics

results for similar key words and bingo! You have a bank of similar ideas, images, et al.

Creative Aerobics is dynamic. The connections you make during the process, the results and solutions you arrive at will be different from another's. Or what you yourself will make at a different point, in a different setting! It allows for originality. The fun process helps you change gear swiftly and get out of freeze mode. And when things are still muddily clear, it offers more clarity. Here's a confession:

I had always enjoyed the classes on Creative Aerobics and looked forward to them when in MICA. But perhaps I didn't quite understand its potential till I got stuck one fine day. At my wit's end, I went back to Creative Aerobics, to the lessons learnt in 2005. And I have never again let go of it!

The fifth and last commentary on CA comes from a highly respected professional/academic who has established a trio of impressive careers.

Sushil Bahl

Professor Sushil Bahl, former President of the Advertising Club of Bombay (1990–91), has over 35 years' experience, in the form of three careers in India: client servicing at JWT and Lowe Lintas; PR and publicity at Tata Group and Mafatlal Group; and academics—teaching marketing and advertising—at Nirma University, Flame University, and International School of Business and Media.

He first observed the concept of CA from Linda Correll George herself, in person, when she was associated with MICA. He has then also been taking his MBA students through the use of CA in the subject of advertising planning ever since.

Having worked on both sides, the ad agency side and the client side, he tries to bring a unique blend of branding and creativity into his classroom teaching, and he himself enjoys the working process of CA:

Creative Aerobics is about unlocking the enormous creativity lying dormant in us marketing and advertising professionals! Using a series of mental exercises that develop the linkage between the left brain and right brain for producing out-of-the box ideas. It is a process-driven technique building on relevant information, leading to multiple ideas for selection and use, which may not have been thought about when using conventional methods.

We are today in the age where lead time for creative ideation and its management is often very short and urgent. We are expected to deliver creativity on demand!

In real life situations, this is not entirely possible.

We can access (google) information on our computers in seconds, but accessing true creativity, we know, takes much longer. Our challenge, therefore, is to speed up, without sacrificing on the quality of our ideas. We need newer methods to be creative and to succeed. Linda Correll George's Creative Aerobics is one such method. The process of using the left brain and right brain, collaborative effort over an individual effort, and mastery over it to enhance the speed of the creativity.

Let us, for instance, consider the need of quickly naming a new and to be launched model of Sony Television using the Creative Aerobics process. First, we select the physical characteristics—the TV set is square, with a large screen, HD quality, etc. We might like to review objects that are square and like to, in the name, project it as a box, big and wide, expansive, entertaining, etc. All relevant to the product. Next, we wish the name to reflect its features and functions, and thus we describe it as a theatre, informative, lifestyle oriented, decorative, stylish, etc. We go further in terms of stating it offers worldwide program content, instant, live, etc. With each step giving us options related and relevant to the suitable and probable name.

Too many ideas? Yes. We may get bogged down and don't know which ideas to work on further in developing them and in order to be able to give the TV model a name.

Creative Aerobics helps us to move from the obvious to the less obvious, from the objective to the subjective, from the intellectual to the intuitive, and from the expected to the unexpected. The more practiced you become at doing the exercise, your focus on the assignment will *improve, the confusion will be resolved, and it will help you to focus on your objective and solution.*

In the case of the name for our model of Sony TV, if we decide on the options in the exercise arising out of rational features of the TV in bringing life into the TV broadcasts in the home, a prospective shortlist of names to choose from may be 'Homevision', 'Worldvision', 'Vistavision', 'Panavision', or 'Spectravision'. After this, the final selection may be taken at a higher level in the organization—by the creative head or director. The logotype and design can follow, within the development of the advertising campaign.

Ideas in our minds come anytime and anywhere! Sometimes even when not needed! But as we have now seen, creativity in advertising is a capacity and a thinking process together! We need to concentrate on the Creative Aerobics process and practice, practice, and practice it to become an expert who delivers creative ideas, on demand! As suggested by author Linda Correll George.

If your left brain is the body of pragmatic work that you do and have done, your right brain is now the soul of the individual, unconventional, and imaginative work you can do and will do using your newly learned tools.

As I said earlier, the work has become, in essence, **you**.

This is the concluding chapter of this book. But it is not the last word, nor is it the end of the discussion of the importance of creativity in the workplace today. It is a conversation that is being conducted all around you—locally, nationally, and globally. And while the language may be foreign, it's meaning is clear—there will never be a better time in business for creativity. And there will never be a better time for you to make creativity your business!

Index

7UP soft drink, 124
.com creativity, 140
   display/banner advertisements, 142
   search pages, 142
   social media, 143
AKA small, 13
apps, 144
audio, 131

Bahl, Sushil, 153
bear with us, 102
Big Idea, The, 13
   bite the bullet, 16
   dimensions, measurement, 18
billboards, 128
BMWs, 113
Boches, Edward, 14
body copy, 81
   lead-in, 86
   rule of thumb, 92
   speaking of style, 93
   wrap-up, 87
Bora Bora ad, 58
Buzan, Tony, 24

camera, 132
Carvalho, Elrid, 151
checkpoint, 80
close-up (CU), 132
Corona beer, 126
couples counseling, 57
Craftsman tools ad, 49
creative aerobic 1 (CA1), 42
   Band-Aid ad, 109

Craftsman tools ad, 49
Crest Whitestrips ad, 50
Dublin, Ireland ad, 49
Heineken ad, 111
MacBook ad, 48
slogan, 122
creative aerobic 2 (CA2), 51
   BMWs, 112
   Bora Bora ad, 58
   Cuisinart ad, 57
   Nike ad, 115
   Oral-B ad, 56
   Petco pet training ad, 57
   slogan, 124
creative aerobic 3 (CA3), 59
   FOSSIL ad, 63
   IRL Printers ad, 116
   Kodak ad, 63
   Lexus ad, 115
   slogan, 125
creative aerobic 4 (CA4), 65
   Minnesota AIDS Line ad, 116
   Scrabble ad, 117
   slogan, 125
creative aerobics (CA), 1
   advantages, 1
   AKA small versus The Big Idea, 13
   creative process, 24
   creativity marathon, training, 39
   exercise, 3, 12
   forward and backward, 10
   magnifying glass, 31
Crest Whitestrips ad, 50
criterion tool, 55
Cuisinart ad, 57

cut, 133
Czech Republic ad, The, 80

Das Auto, 119
de Bono, Edward, 24
directed selection, 55
display/banner advertisements, 142
dissolve, 134
Doors and Windows Company, 16
Dublin, Ireland ad, 49
Duck brand, 142

Esso/Exxon gasoline, 124
establishing shot (ES), 132
extreme close up (ECU), 132

Facebook, 143
footage, 133
FOSSIL ad, 63

Ganguly, Broti, 152
get to the point, 70
Glasnevin cemetery, 49
Google, 66, 143
Guardian, The, 14

Head & Shoulders shampoo, 123
Heineken ad, 111
hoardings, 128
hospitality suite, 17
hunt and peck, 104

Instagram, 143
IRL Printers ad, 116
Ivory soap, 122

Jerome Monroe (JM) Smucker, 123
J. Walter Thompson (JWT), 24

Kodak ad, 63

learning process, 39
Lexus ad, 115

LinkedIn, 143
long shot (LS), 132

MacBook ad, 48
Madrid ad, 79
magnifying glass, 31
mass media
   hoardings, billboards, outdoor boards, transit shelters, 128
   radio commercials, 136
   television
      commercials, 129
      script, creating, 134
      terminology and definitions, 131
McKinsey Quarterly, 32
medium close up (MCU), 132
medium long shot (MLS), 132
medium shot (MS), 132
Minnesota AIDS Line ad, 116
M&M's® candy, 123
Morton salt, 125

Nickelodeon TV, 123
Nike ad, 115

Oral-B ad, 56
outdoor boards, 128

paint store, 79
PAN left, 133
PAN right, 133
Petco pet training ad, 57
phrases, 74
primary research, 31
professional work, 109
   BMWs, 112
   Heineken ad, 111
   IRL Printers ad, 116
   Lexus ad, 115
   Minnesota AIDS Line ad, 116
   Nike ad, 115
   Scrabble ad, 117
profession, practical reflections on, 145
   Carvalho, Elrid, 151

Ganguly, Broti, 152
Venkatraman, Prasad, 149

radio commercials, 136
random selection, 55
random selection tool, 56

Scrabble ad, 117
search pages, 142
secondary research, 31
SHIP safety matches ad, 78
Skittles confectionery, 124
slogan, 119
    CA1, 122
    CA2, 124
    CA3, 125
    CA4, 125
snap zoom, 133
social media, 143
social networking sites, 144
soft cut, 134
state farm, 125
student award winners
    bear with us, 102
    hunt and peck, 104
    natural selection, 96
    survival of the fittest, 103
Surf Excel, 14
survival of the fittest, 103

Taco Bell fast food, 126
Tan, Joo Heng, 15
Technique for Producing Ideas, A, 24
television
    commercials, 130
    script, 135
    terminology and definitions, 131
Tendle, Subhash, 145
toolbox, 55, 57
Twitter, 143

Unilever company, 14

Venkatraman, Prasad, 149
verbal four-/for-/foreplay, 74
    Czech Republic ad, The, 80
    Madrid ad, 79
    SHIP safety matches ad, 78
video, 131

websites, 144
'what-it-isn't' (WII), 51

Young, James Webb, 24
YouTube, 143

zoom in, 133
zoom out, 133

Other SAGE Response titles that might be of interest to you

The inspirational business story of Huawei: how to grow from start up to world leader in two decades.

₹1,250
Hardback
978-93-860-6205-5

An outstanding analysis of the ramifications and ambit of Corporate Governance.

₹595
Paperback
978-93-859-8521-8

A must read for improving interpersonal relations at the workplace, within the family and elsewhere.

₹525
Paperback
978-93-515-0102-2

Young ambitious people need to read Walter's fascinating book to achieve success without waiting for 30 years.

₹295
Paperback
978-93-859-8527-0